Over 600 Definitions for Catholic Kids and Their Parents and Teachers

Written by Janet L. Alampi

Pauline
BOOKS & MEDIA
Boston

Nihil Obstat:
Reverend Thomas W. Buckley, S.T.D., S.S.L.

Imprimatur:
✠ Seán Cardinal O'Malley, O.F.M. Cap.
Archbishop of Boston
August 10, 2007

Library of Congress Cataloging-in-Publication Data
Alampi, Janet L.
  Look it up! : over 600 definitions for Catholic kids and their parents and teachers / written by Janet L.
Alampi.
     p. cm.
  ISBN 0-8198-4523-X (pbk.)
  1. Catholic Church--Dictionaries, Juvenile. I. Title.
  BX841.A53 2007
  282.03--dc22
                         2007031594

Picture Acknowledgements:
Ambiente Socio-Culturale: Dead Sea scrolls, p. 24.
Ann Richard Heady, FSP: crosier, p. 22.
Antonio Achilli: Joseph, p. 47; John the Baptist, p. 47;
   Holy Family, p. 41; Good Shepherd, p. 38; Annunciation, p. 8.
Arturo Mari: zucchetto, p. 80.
Carmita Rodriguez: altar server, p. 7.
Cimabue-Basilica Inferiore de S. Francesco Assisi:
   Franciscans, p. 35.
Conxolus-Subiaco: Benedictines, p. 13.
Daughters of St. Paul: tabernacle, p. 75; confirmation, p. 20;
   censer, p. 17; baptismal font, p. 12; alb, p. 6; chasuble, p. 18;
   Sacred Heart, p. 70; Holy Land, p. 41; Galilee, p. 36;
   Eucharist, p. 30; preparation of the gifts, p. 64; sacramentals,
   p. 69.
G. Pirrone: evangelists (Matthew, Mark, Luke, John), p. 31.
Giovanni Donato da Montorfano: (St. Catherine of Siena)
   doctor of the Church, p. 26.
Hans Memling / La Resurrection du Christ: resurrection,
   p. 67.
H.D.E.: ambo, p. 7.

Hoffmann: halo, p. 40.
International News Photo: visitation, p. 79. Used by
   permission from INP. All rights reserved.
Josephite Fathers: miter, p. 55.
Linda Maria: dalmatic, p. 24, deacon, p. 24.
Mary Emmanuel Alves, FSP: sanctuary lamp, p. 71;
   lector, p. 50; holy orders, p. 42; cruets, p. 23; Eucharist,
   pp. 29, 30.
Mary Joseph Peterson, FSP: chalice, p. 17; ciborium, p. 19;
   font, p. 35; miraculous medal, p. 55; oils, holy, p. 59;
   pall, p. 60; paten, p. 62; purificator, p. 65; pyx, p. 65;
   relic, p. 67; scapular, p. 71; vigil light, p. 78.
Rebecca Horton, OP: Dominicans, p. 27.
Saints, Signs, and Symbols by W. Ellwood Post;
   Morehouse-Barlow Co.,Wilton, CT: Lamb of God, p. 49;
   INRI, p.46; HIS, p. 44; Holy Spirit, p. 42.
Sebastiano del Piombo: memorare, p. 54.
Society of St. Paul: (Icona di Marek Grzegorek,
   Czestochowa) icon, p. 44.

Cover and inside design by Mary Joseph Peterson, FSP

The Scripture quotations contained herein are from the *New Revised Standard Version Bible: Catholic Edition*, copyright © 1989, 1993, Division of Christian Education of the National Council of the Churches of Christ in the United States of America. Used by permission. All rights reserved.

Published by Pauline Books & Media, 50 Saint Pauls Avenue, Boston, MA 02130-3491.

Printed in the U.S.A.

www.pauline.org

Pauline Books & Media is the publishing house of the Daughters of St. Paul, an international congregation of women religious serving the Church with the communications media.

2 3 4 5 6 7 8 9   13 12 11 10 09

To my wonderful husband and terrific children.
I have no words to describe how much they mean to me.

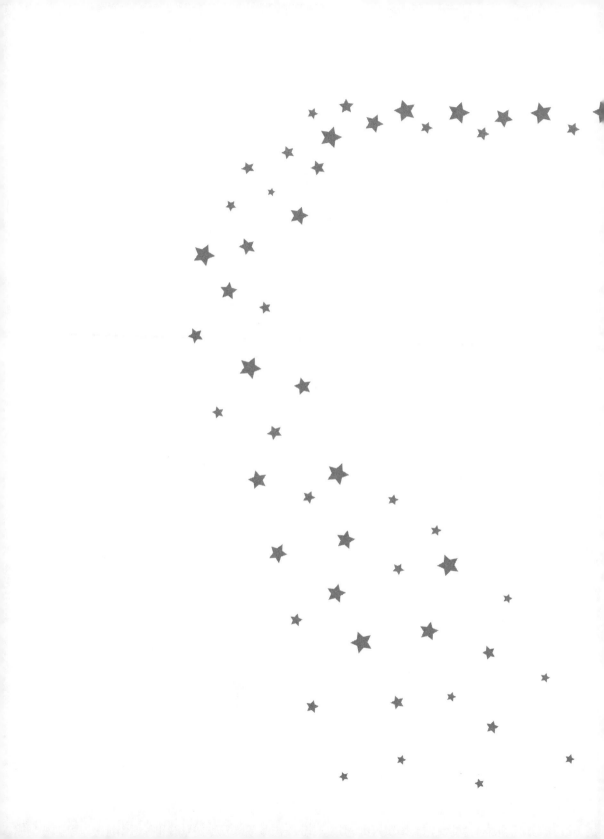

Introduction

Look It Up! is a dictionary for Catholic kids (and their parents and teachers). It will help you to learn more about words that Catholics use. Some of these words are unique to our religion. Others, in addition to religious meanings, have nonreligious meanings and can be found in ordinary dictionaries. *Look It Up!* gives the religious meanings of words.

You probably know that Jesus is called the "Word made flesh" and that the Bible is referred to as "God's word." Words must be very important if "word" is another name for both Jesus and Scripture! According to the Bible, God created everything just by saying the words "Let there be." And Jesus sometimes worked miracles—calmed storms, healed people, raised the dead—merely by speaking.

Think a moment: How are words important in your life?

How could we understand different ideas and communicate with each other if we didn't have words? Whether they're spoken or written, words help us to grasp meanings and build relationships.

Learning the Catholic definitions in *Look It Up!* with its pronunciations, illustrations, "Did You Know?" facts, and the "FYI—For Your Information" section at the end will help you to understand homilies at Mass, classes on the faith, and books that are related to religion. Even more, you'll deepen your appreciation of your Catholic faith and grow closer to Jesus, the Word.

Mastering Catholic terms takes some effort. But so does putting together a puzzle or winning a tough game. Are you up to the challenge? If so, let's *Look It Up!*

How to Use

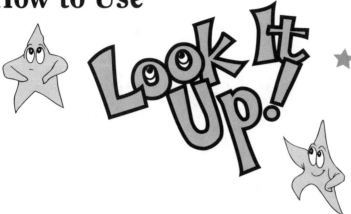

How to look up words in *Look It Up!*

All of the words are arranged in alphabetical order from A to Z so that you can find them easily. Each definition starts out with a new word in bold type. After the word, you will find the word spelled out according to the way it sounds. This will help you say the word correctly. The syllable that is stressed is in capital letters. For example, the first word "Abba" is spoken with the stress on the first syllable (AH-buh).

Watch for guidewords to help you find the correct page. These words are in bold type at the left-hand and right-hand top corners of each page. They indicate the first word on the left-hand page and last word on the right-hand page.

How to find out more about a word

In *Look It Up!* you will discover even more about the word. Many of the definitions have illustrations. For example, the term "Advent wreath" has the definition of the term and also a picture so that you can see what it looks like.

Sometimes a definition may contain other new words that may not be familiar to you. After many of the definitions you will find the words "See (followed by another word in *italics*)." By looking up one new word you may learn about other words as well!

In other places, two words or phrases will have the same definition. For example, "General Intercessions" and "Prayer of the Faithful" mean the same thing. When you look up *General Intercessions* you will not find a definition. Instead, it says, "See *Prayer of the Faithful*," so that you can look for the definition there.

Throughout the book, you will come across "Did You Know?" facts. They give you more interesting information about the new word you are learning. For example, the information box for the word "cross" has explanations of many different types of crosses.

For Your Information

At the end of the book, on page 81, you will find the section "FYI—For Your Information." This section has listings of important topics, such as the Ten Commandments, the Beatitudes, the Sacraments, the Holy Days of Obligation, and so on. These listings provide a helpful reference and are referred to throughout the text.

For parents and teachers

The definitions in *Look It Up!* are doctrinally accurate yet simple enough for intermediate-aged children to understand.

Look It Up! can be used in the home or classroom. As parents, you can use this book with your children to reinforce their religion classes and/or sacramental preparation. You will find this book a helpful aid when your children have questions or assignments on religious subjects. If you homeschool, *Look It Up!* will be a valuable resource in teaching the faith to your children.

Look It Up! is an effective teaching tool for religion teachers and catechists as well. You can use it to keep up-to-date on Catholic words and phrases. You will find just the right definition at your fingertips, along with pronunciations, illustrations, "Did You Know?" facts, cross references, and an appendix with helpful listings of Catholic information. *Look It Up!* is an important addition to your personal, school, or parish library.

Abba (AH-buh) The Aramaic (the language Jesus spoke) word for "father." Jesus called God "Abba."

abbey (AB-ee) The home of monks or nuns. The leader of monks is an abbot; the leader of nuns is an abbess. See *monastery*.

abortion (uh-BOR-shuhn) The deliberate destruction of a fetus, which is an unborn child.

absolution (ab-suh-LOO-shuhn) The forgiveness of sin through the sacrament of Reconciliation when we are truly sorry. The priest says the words of absolution in the name of Jesus, who died so that our sins would be forgiven. We are pardoned through the power Jesus entrusted to the Church. See *general absolution*.

abstinence (AB-stuh-nuhns) Doing without, usually in a spirit of penance. The Church requires that Catholics over the age of fourteen abstain from meat on Ash Wednesday and all Fridays of Lent. See *fasting*.

acclamation (ak-luh-MAY-shun) The people's short prayer in response to the word of God or after the priest's prayer during Mass.

Acts of the Apostles (uh-POS-uhls) An account of the early Church believed to be the continuation of Saint Luke's Gospel. It describes important events such as the Ascension, Pentecost, the conversion of Saul, and the miracles worked through the apostles.

actual grace (AK-choo-uhl) See *grace, actual*.

actual sin See *sin, actual*.

A.D. Abbreviation of the Latin phrase *anno Domini* (in the year of the Lord), which may be written before or after a year to identify it as a year following the birth of Jesus (dated as 0).

Adam The name of the first man as given in the book of Genesis. See *Eve*.

adoption, supernatural (uh-DOP-shun, soo-per-NACH-er-uhl) The spiritual bond between God and human beings, who are brothers and sisters of Christ. We become members of God's family through Baptism.

adoration (ad-uh-RAY-shuhn) Worship; the greatest honor, given only to God. Honor given to Mary is not adoration. It is called *hyperdulia*. Honor given to saints and angels is called *dulia*.

adultery (uh-DUHL-tuh-ree) Sexual intercourse between a married person and someone other than his or her spouse.

5

Adultery breaks the marriage vows by which a person promises to love his or her partner only and forever. It is forbidden by the sixth commandment.

Advent The liturgical season, lasting approximately four weeks, during which the Church prepares for Jesus' coming. Advent means "coming." The season of Advent ends with Christmas, the celebration of Jesus' birth, his coming in history. During Advent we also reflect on Jesus' coming to us every day in mystery as well as on his Second Coming in majesty at the end of time.

Advent wreath (reeth) A circle of evergreen branches (symbolizing God's life that has no end) and four candles, often decorated with bows, that represent the weeks of Advent. Three candles are purple and one is pink. If the candles are white, the bows are purple and pink. On each Sunday of Advent an additional candle is lit and prayers are said. The pink candle is lit on the Third Sunday to express joy that Christmas is near.

advocate (AD-vuh-kit) A person who pleads for another's cause. In the Gospel of John, Jesus calls the Holy Spirit the Advocate. The Holy Spirit stands up for us as a powerful friend and helps us to follow Jesus and his teachings. Mary, the Mother of God, is also our advocate.

age of reason The point at which a person can tell right from wrong and be held responsible for his or her actions. The age of reason is usually reached by the end of the seventh year. Once a Catholic has reached the age of reason, he or she is required to participate at Mass on Sundays and holy days, and to obey other Church laws. The child is also eligible to receive Holy Communion.

agnostic (ag-NOS-tik) Someone who isn't sure whether or not God exists.

Agnus Dei (AG-nuhs DAY-ee) Latin for "Lamb of God." See *Lamb of God*.

agony of Christ The awful mental suffering that Jesus felt in the Garden of Gethsemane on the night before he died as he prayed that the Father's will be done. Jesus' anguish was so great that he sweat blood. But his prayer strengthened him, and through his passion, death, and resurrection, Jesus saved the world.

alb A long, white robe that is worn by ministers of the altar during the eucharistic celebration and other liturgical functions.

All Saints' Day November 1, a feast and a holy day of obligation in the United States (except when it falls on a Saturday or Monday). This feast honors all saints, whether they have been officially canonized or not. Its eve is Halloween, a name derived from Hallowed (Holy Ones) Eve.

All Souls' Day November 2, a day when Catholics pray for those who have died. Mass is offered for the intention of freeing those who might still be in purgatory.

Alleluia (al-lay-LOO-yuh) A prayer that expresses joy in the greatness of God. The word is Hebrew for "Yahweh be praised!" and occurs often in the psalms. Catholics sing "Alleluia" before and after a brief verse, right before the proclamation of the Gospel during the Mass. During Lent the Alleluia is not said.

Almighty (awl-MY-tee) Able to do all things; possessing all powers. Only God is almighty.

alms Gifts of money or goods made to needy people in a spirit of Christian charity. Almsgiving, along with fasting and prayer, is a practice that characterizes the season of Lent.

Alpha and Omega (AL-fuh and oh-MAY-guh) The first (alpha) and last (omega) letters of the Greek alphabet. In Revelation 22:13, Jesus is the Alpha and Omega, the first and the last, the beginning and the end. He is everything from eternity to eternity. The alpha and omega are used in Church art and are also carved into the paschal candle.

Alpha & Omega

altar (AWL-ter) The holy table upon which the sacrifice of Mass is offered and around which God's people gather to share the eucharistic meal. The altar stands for Christ. The relics of saints are often placed in or under the altar.

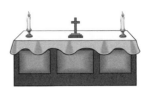

altar cloth The cloth that covers the altar.

altar server A person who assists the priest at the altar during Mass or who helps in other liturgical services.

altar stone A flat piece of stone that contains relics and is embedded in the altar.

ambo (AM-boh) The lectern from which the word of God is proclaimed.

ambry (AM-bree, also spelled aumbry) Wall cupboard in the sanctuary of the church in which holy oils are kept.

amen A Hebrew word that means "yes!" or "truly." Saying "Amen" after a prayer is an expression of one's faith and one's agreement with the prayer.

angels (AYN-jels) Powerful beings created by God who have high intelligence and free will and, like God, are pure spirit. They praise and serve God, sometimes acting as his messengers. Although angels have no bodies, they can assume bodies when appearing on earth. According to tradition, some angels turned against God and became fallen angels. Tradition also holds that there are nine choirs of angels with different tasks. See *guardian angels, archangel, devils, cherubim, seraphim*.

DID YOU KNOW?

The nine choirs of angels are: seraphim, cherubim, thrones, dominions, virtues, powers, archangels, principalities, and angels.

Angelus (AN-juh-luhs) A prayer honoring Mary and the Incarnation, traditionally prayed in the morning, at noon, and in the evening. The Angelus takes its name from its first word in Latin, angelus, which means "the angel." See *Incarnation*.

anger An emotion that can be either good or bad. Anger is a capital sin when it leads to the desire for revenge or actions that harm a person. Anger is just if it leads to good changes through lawful means.

annulment (uh-NUHL-munt) A Church decree stating that two people were not actually married because one of the

requirements for a true marriage was lacking. For example, if the marriage wasn't freely entered into, it would be invalid. An annulment is declared only after a thorough investigation. Persons who have been granted an annulment are free to marry again.

Annunciation (uh-nuhn-see-AY-shuhn) The Angel Gabriel's announcement of the Incarnation to Mary at Nazareth. At Mary's consent, the Son of God became man in her through the power of the Holy Spirit. The feast of the Annunciation is March 25, nine months before Christmas. See *Incarnation*.

anointing (uh-NOINT-ing) Pouring blessed oil on persons, places, or things, to make them holy. Israelites anointed their priests, prophets, and kings. Anointing with oil is used in celebrating the sacraments of Baptism, Confirmation, Anointing of the Sick, and Holy Orders. See *oils, holy*.

Anointing of the Sick A sacrament administered by a priest or bishop to those who are seriously ill, elderly, or in danger of death. Through the blessed oil of the sick and the words of this sacrament, God offers spiritual healing, the

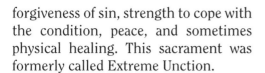

forgiveness of sin, strength to cope with the condition, peace, and sometimes physical healing. This sacrament was formerly called Extreme Unction.

antichrist Jesus Christ's ultimate enemy. According to Scripture, the antichrist will appear shortly before the Second Coming of the Lord.

antiphon (AN-tuh-fon) A short verse, usually from a psalm or other part of the Bible. An antiphon is said or sung before and/or after a psalm or in between its verses.

Apocalypse (uh-POK-uh-lips) See *Revelation, Book of.*

Apocrypha (uh-POK-ruh-fuh) On the one hand, writings that are not included in the Bible because the Church concluded they were not divinely inspired, for example, the Gospel of Thomas. On the other hand, the Catholic Church includes some books in the Bible that Protestants do not, and they call those books the Apocrypha.

apostasy (uh-POS-tuh-see) The rejection of Christian faith by a baptized person who had freely believed.

apostle (uh-POS-uhl) One who is sent and who represents and acts on the authority of the sender. The term is usually applied to the twelve men that Jesus chose as his closest followers. These became witnesses to the resurrection of Jesus, preachers of the Gospel, and leaders of his Church. Today's bishops are their successors. The twelve apostles are Peter, Andrew, James, John, Thomas, James, Philip, Bartholomew (or Nathanael), Matthew, Simon, Jude (Thaddeus), and Matthias, who replaced Judas Iscariot, the betrayer. Saint Paul is called the Apostle to the Gentiles.

Apostles' Creed A prayer from the first centuries of the Church that is a statement of belief, summarizing the teachings of the apostles. The Apostles' Creed has twelve articles (parts) that contain the main beliefs of Christianity. It is handed on as a gift during the Rite of Christian Initiation of Adults.

Apostleship of Prayer (uh-POS-uhl-ship) A worldwide Catholic organization that promotes prayer to the Sacred Heart of Jesus. Members daily pray the Morning Offering for the two intentions the pope assigns for each month.

apostolate (uh-POS-tl-it) Work that the followers of Jesus do today to carry on the mission he entrusted to his apostles—the salvation of the world.

apostolicity (uh-pos-tl-IS-i-tee) One of the four identifying characteristics, or marks, of the true Catholic Church. It has three meanings: (1) The Church is founded on the apostles and shares in the mission Jesus gave them. (2) The pope and bishops—who are lawful successors of the apostles—have the same special authority and responsibilities that Jesus entrusted to the first apostles. (3) Led by the hierarchy, the Church teaches today what Jesus handed on to the apostles to teach.

Apostolic See (ap-uh-STOL-ik) See *Holy See*.

apparition (ap-uh-RISH-uhn) A vision of Jesus, the Blessed Virgin Mary, another saint, or an angel. In the Bible, angels often appeared to people. Today, the Church carefully investigates claims that an apparition has taken place and never declares that it must be believed. Popular approved sites of Marian apparitions are Lourdes, Fatima, and Guadalupe.

Aramaic (ar-uh-MAY-ik) The language spoken by Jesus and most of the Jews during Jesus' life. The New Testament contains several Aramaic words and phrases.

archangel (AHRK-ayn-juhl) A high-ranking angel whom God sends to deliver important messages to people during key times in salvation history. For example, the Archangel Gabriel announced to Mary that God had chosen her to become the mother of the Savior. In the Bible we read that the Archangel Michael and his angels battled with Satan. He is the champion of loyalty to God and the protector of the People of God. The story of the Archangel Raphael, who brought healing to the blind man Tobit and accompanied Tobit's son on his journey, is also found in the Bible.

archbishop (ahrch-BISH-uhp) The bishop of an archdiocese, who usually has some authority over bishops in nearby dioceses.

archdiocese (arch-DY-uh-sees) A territory headed by an archbishop that is the primary diocese in a group of dioceses that form a Church province. See *diocese*.

ark In the Book of Genesis, the large boat that Noah built to save himself, his family, and pairs of  animals during the great flood. God sent forty days of rain to wipe out other life on earth because of sin. The ark is a symbol of the Church, which saves us. See *deluge*.

ark of the covenant (KUHV-uh-nuhnt) The portable wooden box that Moses built to hold the stone tablets containing the commandments. The ark was lined with gold inside and out, and on the top were two angels facing each other. To the Israelites, the ark was the  throne of God and a sign of his presence with them in their desert wanderings and in the first Temple, where the ark was kept in the holy of holies.

articles of faith (AHR-ti-kuhls) Statements of belief about truths revealed by God.

Ascension (uh-SEN-shuhn) The entry of Jesus into heaven forty days after his resurrection when he was exalted at the Father's right hand where he remains in glory. The feast of the Ascension is a holy day of obligation in the United States. It is celebrated either on the Thursday that falls forty days after Easter, or on the nearest Sunday. The bishop of each diocese makes this decision.

Ash Wednesday The first day of Lent. On this day, blessed ashes, obtained by burning the palms used on the previous Palm Sunday, are traced on the foreheads of believers in the form of a cross. Wearing ashes has long been a sign of one's sorrow for sin. The ashes and the words said remind us of death and of the importance of contrition and penance.

assumption (uh-SUHMP-shuhn) The taking up of Mary, the Mother of Jesus, body and soul, into heaven at the end of her earthly life. She is already enjoying the state that awaits the other faithful members of the Church at the end of the world. The feast of the Assumption, celebrated on August 15, is a holy day of obligation in the United States (except when it falls on a Saturday or Monday).

astrology (uh-STROL-uh-jee) The sin of foretelling the future by studying the position of the stars. See *divination*.

atheist (AY-thee-ist) Someone who doesn't believe that God exists.

atonement (uh-TOHN-muhnt) The redemptive act of Jesus that reconciled human beings with God. The word means "at one" again.

auxiliary bishop (awg-ZIL-yuh-ree) See *bishop, auxiliary*.

avarice (AV-er-is) Greed, covetousness, an *extreme* desire for wealth. This capital sin is committed when a person values material goods above everything else, including the welfare of others.

Ave Maria (AH-vay muh-REE-uh) The Latin words for "Hail Mary."

Babel, Tower of (BAB-uhl) A structure that Noah's descendants built. Genesis 11:1–9 tells this story, which is intended to explain the origin of nations and languages. God confused the languages of the people and they scattered to different parts of the earth.

balm The fragrant resin from certain trees that is mixed with oil to make chrism.

banns The public announcement—in speech or writing—that a couple has decided to marry. The purpose of the banns is to find out whether there is any impediment to the marriage. Banns are usually published three times in the parish bulletin.

Baptism (BAP-tiz-uhm) The first and most necessary sacrament of initiation that makes us children of God and members of the Church and gives us the right to receive the other sacraments. It unites us to Christ and, through his death and resurrection, makes us heirs of heaven. At Baptism, a person is freed of original sin as well as any personal sin, and is given sanctifying grace, the theological virtues, and the gifts of the Holy Spirit. The sacrament consists of pouring water on a person or immersing him or her while saying, "I baptize you in the name of the Father, and of the Son, and of the Holy Spirit." In an emergency, anyone can baptize. See *theological virtues*.

Baptism, conditional (kuhn-DISH-uh-nl) Baptism that is administered when there is doubt about whether a person has been validly baptized. The minister prefaces the words of Baptism with "If you are not yet baptized."

Baptism of blood The sacrament of salvation (the removal of sin and granting of sanctifying grace) that is received by someone who dies for the Catholic faith before he or she is able to be baptized with water.

Baptism of desire The sacrament of salvation that is received by someone who intends to seek God and do God's will and is sorry for sin but who is unable to be baptized with water.

baptismal font (bap-TIZ-muhl) A basin or pool that is used for baptisms.

baptistery (BAP-tuh-stree) A building separate from the church or the part of the church that is used for baptisms.

basilica (buh-SIL-i-kuh) An especially important church. Major basilicas are located in Rome; minor basilicas are found there and elsewhere.

B.C. Abbreviation for "before Christ." The years *before* the birth of Jesus (dated as 0) are preceded or followed by "B.C."

beatification (bee-at-uh-fi-KAY-shuhn) The last step before a person is declared a saint. The pope beatifies a person after his or her writings, teaching, and life are carefully studied and found to be worthy, and after a miracle has been worked through the person's intercession. Once beatified, a person is called Blessed and can be publicly honored in Church celebrations. See *canonization*.

beatific vision (bee-uh-TIF-ik) The clear knowledge of God enjoyed by those who are in heaven and see God face to face as he is. While on earth, we know God through our faith and minds and creation. Those in heaven know God directly, and this bond brings complete happiness. *Beatific* means causing perfect happiness.

Beatitudes (bee-AT-uh-toohdz) Promises made by Jesus that form a blueprint for Christian living, a way that we can achieve the fullness of life and happiness. In Matthew's Gospel, Jesus gives eight Beatitudes during the Sermon on the Mount. In Luke's Gospel, he gives four Beatitudes. *See p. 82 for a list of the Beatitudes.*

Beelzebub (bee-EL-zuh-buhb) Another name for Satan or anyone who does his work. In Matthew 12:24, Beelzebub means the "prince of demons."

belief The act of faith in which a person accepts certain truths revealed by God.

Benedictines (ben-i-DIK-tins) The religious order founded by Saint Benedict in the sixth century that became the foundation of Western monasticism (the way of life for monks and nuns). The Benedictine Rule combines prayer and work. See *monk, nun*.

St. Benedict, founder of the Benedictines

Benediction (ben-i-DIK-shun) A blessing, in particular the act of blessing people with the Holy Eucharist after exposition of the Blessed Sacrament. See *exposition of the Blessed Sacrament*.

Bethlehem (BETH-li-hem) A town in Israel not far from Jerusalem where King David and his descendant Jesus Christ were born. Bethlehem means "House of Bread."

Bible The collection of various kinds of books written by human beings under the inspiration of God, who is the author. The Bible, also known as Sacred Scripture, has two major parts: the Old Testament, composed of forty-six books, and the New Testament, composed of twenty-seven books. Along with Sacred Tradition, the Bible is the source of God's revelation to human beings. See *Tradition, Sacred. See p. 87 for a list of books in the Bible.*

biretta (buh-RET-uh) A ceremonial cap worn by priests, bishops, and cardinals for special occasions. Since Vatican II, its use has become less common.

birth control See *contraception*.

bishop A successor of the apostles who usually is the head of a diocese and presides at its cathedral. A bishop has received the fullness of the priesthood and can administer all the sacraments. He is assisted by priests and deacons as he serves as Christ did—teaching, governing, and sanctifying. The pope is the bishop of Rome.

bishop, auxiliary (awg-ZIL-yuh-ree) A bishop who assists the diocesan bishop in caring for the people of a certain area.

blasphemy (BLAS-fuh-mee) Hateful, irreverent, defiant language directed to God, the Church, the saints, and holy things. Using God's name to cover up a crime or for some other evil purpose is also blasphemy. Blasphemy is a grave sin against the second commandment.

blessed (1) Holy. (2) Made sacred through a religious rite. (3) The saints. 4) The title given by the pope to a person who has been beatified, the step before canonization.

Blessed Sacrament The Holy Eucharist; the consecrated bread and wine that have become the Body and Blood of Jesus Christ in the Mass. See *Eucharist*.

Blessed Trinity See *Trinity, Holy*.

Blessed Virgin Mary See *Mary, Blessed Virgin*.

blessing The sacramental that asks God's favor, assistance, and grace upon a person or object. The words can be accompanied by outstretched hands, the laying on of hands, the sign of the cross, or the sprinkling of holy water. Blessings are usually imparted by an ordained minister, but some can also be given by a layperson. The official *Book of Blessings* contains many rites for blessings. See *sacramental, rite*.

Blood of Christ Jesus shed his blood to redeem us from sin. See *Eucharist*.

Body of Christ (1) The Eucharist. (2) A name for the Church (sometimes called Mystical Body of Christ) that highlights our union with Jesus. As members of the Church, we are joined to Jesus and to one another, forming one "body" with Jesus as the head. The Mystical Body includes members of the Church on earth, in purgatory, and in heaven.

Bread of Life The expression Jesus used to identify himself in John 6:35. Jesus told a crowd that he would give them himself to eat. He was talking about the Holy Eucharist, but his listeners, who did not understand, murmured and argued about his statements. Still, Jesus said: "This is the bread that came down from heaven, not like that which your ancestors ate, and they died. But the one who eats this bread will live forever" (John 6:58).

Breviary (BREE-vee-er-ee) The book containing the Liturgy of the Hours, or Divine Office. See *Liturgy of the Hours*.

brothers, religious Men in a religious community who make vows but are not ordained.

brothers and sisters of Jesus A phrase in the Gospels that refers to close relatives (such as cousins) of Jesus.

call See *vocation*.

Calvary (KAL-vuh-ree) The hill outside the wall of Jerusalem where Jesus died on the cross. The name is from the Latin term for "place of the skull."

Cana (KAY-nuh) The small town where Jesus attended a wedding and worked his first public miracle at Mary's urging—changing water into wine to save the newlyweds from embarrassment. In Cana, Jesus also healed an official's son.

canon In general, "canon" means a rule or measure and is used in different ways. For example, the canon of Scripture is the list of the books of the Bible. Canon law contains laws of the Church. The canon of the Mass is the Eucharistic Prayer.

canon law See *Code of Canon Law*.

canonization (kan-uh-ni-ZAY-shun) The Church's formal declaration that a deceased person is a saint and may be honored as a model and intercessor. It must be proved that the person prac-ticed heroic virtue or was a martyr. First, the local bishop sends evidence to the Congregation for the Causes of Saints in Rome. If accepted, someone writes a biography, which experts then study. If they approve, the cause goes to the pope. If he approves, the person is declared Venerable. Then, if a miracle is worked, the person is called Blessed. (Martyrs need no miracles.) After more study and another miracle, the pope may declare the person a saint.

canticle (KAN-ti-kuhl) A sacred chant or song other than a psalm that is used in liturgical prayer.

capital sins See *sins, capital*.

cardinal (KAHR-dn-l) A bishop, archbishop or priest chosen by the pope to work closely with him as a member of the College of Cardinals. Cardinals are second in rank to the pope and have the task of electing a pope. They may wear a special red hat and cassock.

cardinal virtues From the Latin *cardo* for hinge, the cardinal virtues are prudence, justice, temperance, and fortitude. Christian virtue depends or hinges on these key virtues.

St. John of the Cross and St. Teresa of Avila were Carmelites

Carmelites (CAR-muh-lyts) A Roman Catholic religious order founded in the twelfth century on Mount Carmel in Israel. Their spirituality focuses on contemplative prayer. The Third Order of Carmelites is made up of laypeople following Carmelite spirituality. See *contemplation*.

cassock (KAS-uhk) An ankle-length robe worn by the clergy.

catacombs (KAT-uh-kohms) Underground tunnels with wall recesses that the early Christians frequently used for burial. The catacombs became places to honor the martyrs.

catechism (KAT-i-kiz-uhm) A book that explains the main truths of the Catholic faith, often in question-and-answer form. The *Baltimore Catechism*, published by the American bishops in 1885, was the standard book for religious education for many years.

Catechism of the Catholic Church A book that explains the truths of the Catholic faith related to the creed, the liturgy, morality, and prayer. Pope John Paul II commissioned the writing of this catechism, which was published in 1992. In 2006, the United States bishops published a national catechism for adults based on this catechism.

catechist (KAT-i-kist) A person who shares the faith with others through teaching and personal witness.

catechumen (kat-i-KYOO-muhn) An adult in the preparation program for becoming a member of the Church. Catechumens study, pray, and are supported by a parish community as they get ready to receive the three sacraments of initiation: Baptism, Confirmation, and Holy Eucharist. See *Rite of Christian Initiation of Adults*.

cathedral (kuh-THEE-druhl) The main church in a diocese and its bishop's official church. The bishop's or archbishop's chair is found in the cathedral. In fact, the word *cathedral* comes from the Greek and Latin words for "chair." In ancient times, the chair stood for its owner's teaching authority.

Catholic Describes the members, teachings, and organizations of the Church that Jesus Christ founded, which is governed by the pope in Rome.

catholicity (kath-uh-LIS-i-tee) An identifying mark or characteristic of the true Church that means that the Church teaches the whole message of Christ and is open to people of all places and all times. No one culture, race, or nation "owns" the Catholic Church. Instead, it welcomes all people who want to follow Jesus Christ. The word *catholic* means "universal."

celebrant (SEL-uh-bruhnt) A member of the clergy (bishop, priest, or deacon) who leads a liturgical celebration.

celibacy (SEL-uh-buh-see) In reference to religion, celibacy means to give up marriage for the sake of the kingdom of God. Celibacy is required of priests in the Latin Rite.

censer (SEN-ser) A small metal container that holds hot coals upon which incense is placed during liturgies. It has a lid to contain the smoke  and swings on chains. A censer is also called a *thurible*. See *incense*.

centering prayer A form of prayer in which we focus on God dwelling within us and use a word or phrase to call our attention back when our minds wander.

Chair of Saint Peter A throne in Saint Peter's Basilica in Rome that is said to contain some pieces of the actual chair used by Saint Peter, the first pope. The chair stood for its owner's teaching authority. The feast of the Chair of Peter on February 22 celebrates the authority of Saint Peter.

chalice (CHAL-is) A sacred cup, often lined with gold, used to hold the Blood of Christ in the celebration of the Eucharist.

chancellor (CHAN-suh-ler) A person who assists the bishop in running the diocese.

chancery (CHAN-suh-ree) The administrative offices of a diocese, including the bishop's office.

Chanukah (KHAH-nuh-kuh) See *Hanukkah*.

chapel A place of worship, usually smaller than a parish church.

chaplain (CHAP-lin) A priest who cares for the spiritual needs of a particular group of people, such as those in a hospital or members of the military.

character, sacramental (KAR-ik-ter, sak-ruh-MEN-tl) See *sacramental character*.

charism (KAR-iz-uhm) A special gift of grace that is given to one person by God but is meant to benefit the members of the Church and meet the needs of the world. It is also referred to as a charismatic gift. *Charism* is related to the Greek word for "free gift." Every religious congregation has a charism shared by each of its members.

DID YOU KNOW?

Saint Paul lists some of the charismatic gifts in his Letter to the Corinthians: "To each is given the manifestation of the Spirit for the common good. To one is given through the Spirit the utterance of wisdom, and to another the utterance of knowledge according to the same Spirit, to another faith by the same spirit, to another gifts of healing by the one Spirit, to another the working of miracles, to another prophecy, to another the discernment of spirits, to another various kinds of tongues, to another the interpretation of tongues" (1 Corinthians 12:7–10).

charity (CHAIR-i-tee) The supernatural, theological virtue by which a person loves God and others for God's sake. Charity, the highest of all virtues and the source of all goodness, enables us to love God above all things and love our neighbor as ourselves. Love is the greatest commandment and the definition of God in the First Letter of John.

charms Objects, words, and gestures that are supposed to have magical powers to ward off evil or bring about good luck. The first commandment forbids such superstition.

chastity (CHAS-ti-tee) The virtue that guides a person's thoughts, actions, and desires in regard to sexual matters. Chaste persons are characterized by purity, modesty, and decency. They show respect for others and for themselves.

chasuble (CHAZ-uh-buhl) The celebrant's outer vestment. The color of the chasuble depends upon the liturgical season or feast.

cherubim (CHER-uh-bim) The second highest of the nine choirs of angels. Cherubim are close to God's glory and serve God. In the Bible, they guarded the Garden of Eden, and two images of them were positioned on the top of the ark of the covenant. See *angels, seraphim*.

chi-rho (KEE-roh) The monogram for Jesus formed by the first two Greek letters in the word "Christ": "chi" (an X) and "rho" (a P). The X is placed on the lower part of the P.

choir (kwyr) (1) A group who are lead singers for liturgical celebrations. (2) The place from which liturgical singers sing. (3) One of the groups (orders) of angels.

chrism (KRIZ-uhm) Perfumed oil used in administering the sacraments of Baptism, Confirmation, and Holy Orders and in giving certain blessings. Chrism is blessed by the bishop at the Mass of the Chrism during Holy Week. It represents the gift of the Holy Spirit. The Eastern Churches call chrism *myron*.

Christ A title for Jesus that is from the Greek word *christos*, meaning "messiah" or "anointed one." It is not really his last name. Because Jesus perfectly fulfilled his mission as king, priest, and prophet, the title "Christ" rightly belongs to him, the one sent by the Father to save the world.

Christendom (KRIS-uhn-duhm) Christianity.

christening (KRIS-uh-ning) A baptism.

Christian (KRIS-chuhn) One who believes in Christ and follows his teachings.

Christianity (kris-chee-AN-i-tee) The religion based on the teachings of Jesus of Nazareth. Members of the Roman Catholic, Orthodox, Anglican, and Protestant faiths as well as other groups are known as Christians.

Christmas The feast celebrating the birth of Jesus. The word *Christmas* is a combination of the words *Christ* and *Mass*. We celebrate Christmas on December 25.

Church (1) The Catholic Church, founded by Jesus Christ on the apostles and composed of all believers on earth, the souls in purgatory, and the saints in heaven, all united in Christ. (2) People in a particular diocese or parish.

church A building dedicated to the worship of God.

ciborium (si-BOR-ee-uhm) A covered container, usually lined with gold, which contains the consecrated Hosts. The ciborium is used for distribution of Communion and afterwards is returned to the tabernacle.

cincture (sink-CHER) A rope-like belt worn over the alb. See *alb*.

clergy (KLUR-jee) Men who have been ordained as deacons, priests, or bishops.

cloister (KLOI-ster) An area of a monastery that is reserved for the religious brothers or sisters who live there.

Code of Canon Law The book of rules used worldwide in the Catholic Church. It was last revised in 1983.

commandments of God The ten laws God revealed to Moses on Mount Sinai and wrote on two stone tablets. The first three commandments have to do with our relationship with God. The last seven have to do with our relationships with people. All the commandments are aimed at helping us find peace on earth and happiness in heaven. Jesus stated that

keeping the commandments is the way to attain eternal life. The commandments are also called the Decalogue. *See p. 82 for a listing of the Ten Commandments.*

commandments of the Church See *precepts of the Church.*

Communion, Holy (kuh-MYOON-yuhn) (1) The Body and Blood of Jesus Christ received during the Eucharistic Celebration. (2) Reception of Jesus truly present under the forms of bread and wine. In Communion, we are united with Jesus and with one another and become more like Jesus. Any baptized Catholic who is free from mortal sin and has fasted an hour from food and drink (water and medicine are permitted any time) may receive Communion. See *Eucharist, Eucharistic celebration.*

communion, spiritual (SPIR-i-choo-uhl) A prayer expressing the desire to receive Communion when it isn't possible.

Communion of Saints The spiritual union that exists among these members of the Church: believers on earth, the souls in purgatory, and the saints in heaven.

conclave (KON-klayv) The very private meetings in which the cardinals elect a new pope. During the time of the conclave, no outsiders are permitted to have contact with the cardinals.

concupiscence (kon-KYOO-pi-suhns) The disordered inclinations that lead us to sin as a result of original sin. We still have concupiscence after we are baptized.

confession (kuhn-FESH-uhn) Admitting one's sins to a priest in order to receive absolution. See *Reconciliation, sacrament of; absolution.*

confessional (kuhn-FESH-uh-nl) An enclosed area for celebrating the sacrament of Reconciliation. The confessional includes a kneeler for the penitent, a screen to conceal the person's identity, and a chair for the priest. Today many parishes use Reconciliation rooms, which allow the penitent the option of using the traditional confessional or of speaking face-to-face with the priest.

confessor (1) A priest who is authorized to hear confessions. (2) An early Christian who suffered for confessing (declaring) the faith but was not martyred. (3) Today a term for any non-martyr saint.

Confirmation (kon-fer-MAY-shuhn) A sacrament of initiation that completes the grace of Baptism and is usually administered by a bishop. It consists of the laying on of hands, anointing on the forehead with chrism, and prayer. The words of Confirmation are "(*Name*), be sealed with the gift of the Holy Spirit." In Confirmation, a person is united more closely to Christ and the Church, and the gifts of the Holy Spirit are deepened. Confirmation strengthens those who receive it to live the faith and become more active members in the Church. The Eastern Churches call this sacrament *chrismation*.

Confraternity of Christian Doctrine (CCD) (kon-fruh-TUR-ni-tee) (1) Originally, a society formed in the sixteenth century to teach religion to children and adults, CCD today refers to the religious education program of a parish. (2) Commonly used to refer to religious education programs for children who do not attend Catholic schools, also known as Parish School of Religion (PSR) programs.

conscience (KON-shuhns) The judgment of our mind as to what is right and wrong, based on faith and reason. A good conscience judges according to correct thinking and the teachings of the Church. Consciences are formed by learning more about the faith and by associating with good people.

consecration (kon-si-KRAY-shuhn) (1) The words Jesus said at the institution of the Eucharist and repeated by the priest during the eucharistic prayer when bread and wine become the Body and Blood of Jesus Christ. (2) The part of the Mass when the bread and wine become the Body and Blood of Jesus. (3) The act or ceremony of setting apart a person for religious service or a thing for sacred use. (4) An act of devotion in which one surrenders oneself to Jesus or Mary as a gift.

contemplation (kon-tuhm-PLAY-shuhn) The highest form of prayer in which we simply gaze wordlessly on God with wonder, adoration, and love.

contraception (kon-truh-SEP-shuhn) The use of pills, drugs, or other means to prevent conception. The Church teaches that this is wrong because it separates married love from the act of giving life.

Contrition (kon-TRI-shuhn) Sorrow for sin, linked with trust in the mercy of God and the decision not to sin again. It can be motivated by fear of punishment (imperfect contrition) or love of God (perfect contrition). Contrition is required in order to be forgiven.

convent The home of religious sisters.

convert (1) One who becomes a member of the Catholic Church after having belonged to a non-Christian religion. (2) To change from sinful ways to the path of virtue. Every Catholic is called to this type of conversion. See *Rite of Christian Initiation for Adults*.

corporal (KOR-per-uhl) (1) Having to do with the body. (2) A square piece of white cloth on which are placed the bread and wine during Mass, the ciborium in the tabernacle, and the monstrance during eucharistic adoration and Benediction. See *ciborium, monstrance, Benediction*.

corporal works of mercy Seven acts of kindness that show respect for the bodies of other human beings by relieving their physical needs. Corporal works of mercy are performed out of love for God and neighbor. In the Gospel of Matthew, chapter 25, Jesus explains that at the last judgment people will be judged on six of these works. *See p. 84 for a list of the corporal works of mercy.*

Corpus Christi (KOR-puhs KRIS-tee) The Latin term for "Body of Christ" and the older name for the feast of the Body and Blood of the Lord, which is celebrated on the Sunday after Trinity Sunday in the United States and Canada.

Council (KOUN-suhl) Church councils can be a meeting of a local church, such as a parish council, or a meeting of bishops from a certain region or from all over the world, such as an ecumenical council. See *Second Vatican Council.*

counsel (KOUN-suhl) The gift of the Holy Spirit that leads one to seek and be open to good advice when making a decision, as well as being able to give good advice. Counsel is sometimes called right judgment.

covenant (KUHV-uh-nuhnt) A solemn agreement between God and human beings. The Old Covenant was made between God and the Israelites at Mount Sinai when God agreed to be their God and the Israelites agreed to obey him. The New Covenant between God and his people was established by Jesus Christ in the sacrifice of his suffering and death. This sacrifice of Jesus reconciled humanity with God and set up a new relationship between them.

covet (KUHV-it) To crave or desire strongly what belongs to another person.

creation (kree-AY-shuhn) (1) The process by which God made all things from nothing out of love for us. (2) Everything that was made by God and that reveals him and his characteristics. Jesus brought about a new creation.

Creator (kree-AY-ter) God, the only Being who can make things from nothing.

creature (KREE-cher) Any person or other living being made by God.

credence table (KREED-ns) The side table that holds the chalice, paten, cruets, dish for the handwashing, purificators, and anything else needed for Mass. See *chalice, paten, cruets, purificators.*

creed A statement of beliefs such as the Apostles' Creed and the Nicene Creed, which is prayed at Mass. See *Apostles' Creed, Nicene Creed.*

crosier (KROH-zher) The staff of bishops and abbots that represents their role of shepherd among the "flock" of Christ.

cross (1) The T-shaped wooden beams Jesus was nailed to and on which he suffered and died to save the world. The cross is now a symbol of the Christian faith. (2) Any pain or suffering that a Christian endures that can be united with the suffering of Jesus to help save the world. Jesus said that his disciples must take up their cross and follow him.

crucifix (KROO-suh-fiks) A cross with the likeness of Jesus on it. Catholics often display crucifixes in their homes and institutions and wear them on a chain around their necks. In church, a crucifix must be near the altar. It is also carried in procession.

crucifixion (kroo-suh-FIK-shuhn) The method of execution in which a person's feet and hands were nailed or tied to a cross. The crucified person suffered a great deal before dying.

cruets (KROO-its) The small containers that hold the water and wine used at Mass.

Crusades (kroo-SAYDZ) Military expeditions between 1096 and 1270 ordered by the popes and undertaken for a religious purpose, primarily to regain the Holy Land from the Muslims. The word *crusade* comes from *crux*, the Latin word for "cross," because the crusaders' clothes and pennants bore crosses.

cursing The act of calling down evil on someone. This is forbidden because Jesus commands people to love one another.

Did You Know?

The traditional cross is the form used in our images of the crucifixion of Christ. It is also called the **Latin** cross. There are other Christian styles of the cross: the **Andrew** cross is shaped like the letter X, the form of cross on which Saint Andrew was martyred; the **Anthony** cross, also called the **Tau** cross, shaped like the letter T, was actually the historical form used by Romans for crucifixion (not the Latin cross). The **Celtic** cross, also known as the **Irish** cross, is basically a Latin cross with a circle. The **Greek** cross has arms of the same length. The **Jerusalem** cross, also known as the **Crusaders'** cross, has four smaller crosses—representing the four evangelists—inserted into the larger cross. The **Orthodox** cross has two more crossbeams than the Latin cross (three crossbeams in all). There are many other forms of Christian crosses.

dalmatic (dal-MAT-ik)
A vestment with wide sleeves, similar to a chasuble. The dalmatic is worn by the deacon at liturgical celebrations. See *chasuble*.

deacon (DEE-kuhn) A man who has received the first level of Holy Orders (the diaconate) and is committed to serving, especially by helping bishops and priests. *Deacon* is from the Greek word for "servant." There are two kinds of deacons: (1) a transitional deacon, who is preparing to receive the next level of Holy Orders and become a priest, and (2) a permanent deacon, who will remain at this level. A permanent deacon  must be at least thirty-five years old and may be married. Among other things, deacons baptize, assist during liturgies, read the Gospel and preach at Mass, assist at and bless marriages, preside at funerals, and perform acts of charity. During the liturgy, a deacon wears a stole draped over his left shoulder.

Dead Sea Scrolls Manuscripts discovered in caves near the Dead Sea from 1947 on. They contain almost all the books of the Hebrew Bible and are mainly written in Hebrew and Aramaic. Enclosed in jars, the scrolls seem to be from the li-

brary of the Essenes, a Jewish monastic community at Qumran from 150 B.C. to A.D. 70.

death The separation of soul and body. The body of a human being becomes lifeless while the soul continues to live.

decade (DEK-ayd) A portion of the rosary that includes one Our Father, ten Hail Marys, and the Glory Be.

Decalogue (DEK-uh-log) Another name for the Ten Commandments. *Decalogue* is from the Greek for "ten sayings." See *commandments of God*.

deluge (DEL-yooj) The great flood in Genesis that destroyed the world except for Noah, his family, and two of each of the animals. God promised Noah and all living creatures that he would never do this again, and he set a rainbow in the sky as a sign of this covenant. See *ark*.

demon A devil, an evil spirit, one of the angels who disobeyed God and who hates human beings. Jesus cast out demons from people who were possessed or affected by them.

Deposit of Faith (di-POZ-it) The treasure of truth revealed by God, given by Jesus to the apostles, and contained in the Bible and Sacred Tradition. The Church tries to remain faithful to these teachings, to understand them better, to proclaim them, and to pass them on through the ages. See *Tradition, Sacred*.

despair The sin committed when a person decides that even God cannot save him or her. Despair is the opposite of hope, through which a person trusts that God is good and cares for all his creatures. A person who despairs has freely decided that God is not trustworthy. Despair is not the same as fear or worry.

detraction The sin of ruining someone's reputation by revealing truths about him or her without good reason. An example of a good reason for revealing negative truths about someone would be to warn another person of danger.

devils "Fallen angels," who, under Lucifer's leadership, chose to disobey God. After losing a war against angels led by Saint Michael, an archangel, the devils were cast down to hell. Devils are evil. Because they hate God and don't want people to be happy on earth or in heaven, devils tempt us to disobey God.

devotion (1) A desire to serve God. (2) Reverence in prayer. (3) A prayer or practices performed to honor God, Mary, or a saint.

diocese (DY-uh-sees) A part of the Church composed of Catholics within a certain geographical area. A diocese or archdiocese has its own bishop or archbishop (and perhaps auxiliary bishops), with priests, deacons, parishes, and offices.

discernment (di-SURN-muhnt) The process of trying to make a decision by taking into consideration God's will. People discern their vocations and other major life changes.

disciple (di-SY-puhl) A student or follower of a teacher. In the Gospels, disciples are all the men and women who received special instruction from Jesus. They formed the early Church and spread the Good News. Today all people who try to follow Christ's teachings are his disciples.

dispensation (dis-pen-SAY-shuhn) A permission that frees a person from keeping a certain law of the Church, such as an obligation to fast. Dispensations cannot be given from God's laws, namely, the Ten Commandments, for the Church cannot give anyone permission to disobey God's law.

divination (div-uh-NAY-shuhn) Superstitious practices carried out for the purpose of gaining information, especially about the future. Examples include crystal balls, ouija boards, horoscopes, palm reading, contacting the dead, and tarot cards. These practices are forbidden by the first commandment because they are appealing to Satan for knowledge that belongs only to God. They show a lack of trust in God's love.

Divine Office See *Liturgy of the Hours*.

Divine Praises A litany recited or sung at the end of Benediction in which we honor the Holy Trinity, Mary, Joseph, the angels and saints. It can be traced to the eighteenth century when a Jesuit, Luigi Felici, encouraged people to pray the Divine Praises to make reparation for sins of blasphemy. See *Benediction, blasphemy, litany*.

divine providence (di-VYN PROV-i-duhns) God's care and concern for creation, keeping it in existence and overseeing his loving and wise plan for it.

divinity of Christ (di-VIN-i-tee) The truth that Jesus Christ, born of Mary, is God the Son, equal to the Father and to the Holy Spirit.

divorce (di-VOHRS) A legal decree that a

marriage has ended. In the eyes of the Church, this decree does not end a valid marriage. The sacrament of Matrimony creates a lifelong bond between a husband and a wife.

doctor of the Church A renowned teacher whose writings and holiness have helped the whole Church. Only thirty-three people have received this title.

DID YOU KNOW?

Of the thirty-three doctors of the Church, three are women: Saint Teresa of Avila, a great mystic, writer, and reformer of her Carmelite Order; Saint Catherine of Siena, a lay member of the Dominican Order, also a mystic and writer, who was an adviser to the popes; and Saint Thérèse of Lisieux, a cloistered Carmelite who became well known through her autobiography, **Story of a Soul**.

St. Catherine of Siena

doctrine (DOK-trin) The beliefs and teachings of the Catholic Church.

dogma A solemnly defined teaching of the Church concerning faith or morals that is revealed by God and held to be infallible. All Catholics are required to believe such a truth. See *infallibility*.

Dominicans (duh-MIN-i-kuhns) Members of the Order of Preachers, founded by Saint Dominic in the thirteenth century. The Dominican family includes multiple branches of priests, religious brothers, contemplative nuns, congregations of contemplative and apostolic sisters, and laypersons.

St. Dominic, founder of the Dominicans

doxology (dok-SOL-uh-jee) A prayer praising the Blessed Trinity. The greater doxology is the "Glory to God" (Gloria) prayer in the Mass; the lesser doxology is the prayer "Glory to the Father."

Easter The greatest feast of the Church year that celebrates the resurrection of Jesus. Easter occurs on the first Sunday after the full moon following the spring equinox (the date in spring when day and night become equal in length). Every Sunday is like a little Easter.

Easter duty See *paschal precept*.

Easter season The fifty-day period in the Church year when we celebrate Christ's resurrection. The Easter season begins with Easter Sunday and ends with the feast of Pentecost.

Easter triduum (TRID-oo-uhm) The three-day celebration of the paschal mystery that begins with the Mass of the Lord's Supper on Holy Thursday and ends with evening prayer on Easter Sunday.

Easter Vigil The Saturday evening before Easter when the resurrection of Jesus Christ is celebrated. The service consists of four parts: the Service of Light, the Liturgy of the Word, Christian Initiation and the Renewal of Baptismal Vows, and the Liturgy of the Eucharist.

At the beginning of the Easter Vigil, the unlit church is transformed by kindling the Easter fire and lighting the paschal candle, signifying that the darkness of sin is replaced by the light of salvation and hope brought by Jesus' resurrection. During this vigil, several Scripture passages are read, holy water is blessed, catechumens and candidates receive the sacraments of initiation, and those in the congregation renew their baptismal vows. See *catechumen*.

Eastern Churches Those groups of Catholics who can trace their origin to Jerusalem, Alexandria, Constantinople, or Antioch. Eastern Catholic beliefs, sacramental system, and moral teachings are the same as the Western (Latin) Churches, and they are in union with Rome. However, members of the Eastern Churches have different rites and practices. Their history is filled with mysticism, symbolism, and a deep sense of God's greatness. Most Eastern Rite Churches have Orthodox (non-Catholic) counterparts. See *Orthodox, mystic*.

ecclesiastical (eh-klee-zee-AS-ti-kuhl) This term is used to describe a person or thing that is related to the Church.

ecstasy (EK-stuh-see) A state of mind and heart in which the Holy Spirit gives a person a special sense of joy and union with God. Some saints experienced ecstasies during their prayer. They were not aware of anything else around them during that time.

ecumenical council (ek-yoo-MEN-i-kuhl) A solemn, official meeting of bishops from around the world, who are called together by the pope. These meetings are usually held at crucial times in the history of the Church. An ecumenical council, joined with the Holy Father, is the Church's highest teaching authority.

ecumenism (EK-yoo-muh-niz-uhm) The movement among Christians and Christian denominations to become united as Jesus wills. While all Christians originally belonged to only one Church, now there are many divisions. Through ecumenism, Christians use various activities, discussions, and prayers to resolve these differences, understand each other better, and collaborate in doing good works.

Eden, Garden of A place filled with beauty and happiness where God put Adam and Eve. They were cast out of Eden after they sinned. See *Adam, Eve*.

Emmanuel (i-MAN-yoo-uhl) A title for Jesus that means "God with us."

encyclical (en-SIK-li-kuhl) An official letter from the pope that contains teachings about a religious topic. An encyclical is usually addressed to the whole Church.

end of the world The unknown time when Christ will return in glory and the last judgment of all people will take place. See *judgment, general*.

envy (EN-vee) The sin of being miserable when another person does well or owns something. An envious person believes that the success of others deprives him or her of happiness and good fortune. Envy is one of the capital sins.

Epiphany (i-PIF-uh-nee) The feast that honors the Magi's visit to Baby Jesus when they presented him with gifts of gold, frankincense, and myrrh. We assume there were three Magi because three gifts are mentioned. Because these wise men had come from the Far East to pay homage to Jesus and were Gentiles, not Jews, they represented the whole world. In the Epiphany, Jesus showed that he was the Savior of all people. In the United States, we celebrate Epiphany on the Sunday between January 2 and January 8.

epistle (i-PIS-uhl) One of the twenty-one letters in the New Testament mostly written by Saint Paul to the early Christian churches. The epistles were written under the inspiration of God to teach about various topics and to encourage the new Christians to live the faith.

eternity (i-TUR-ni-tee) (1) Existence without beginning or end. Only God enjoys the fullness of eternity. Everyone else had a beginning. Time is within eternity. (2) Commonly used to refer to existence that lasts forever: perfect, unending life.

Eucharist (YOO-kuh-rist) Jesus Christ, in his body, blood, soul, and divinity, truly present in this sacrament under the appearances of bread and wine. He will remain with us until the end of the world. Jesus instituted (that is, he established) this sacrament at the Last Supper, surrounded by his twelve apostles. The Eucharist has two aspects: in this *memorial meal* we receive the consecrated bread and wine (Holy Communion) that unites us with Jesus and all others who share in the sacrament. It increases our faith and is a preview of the heavenly banquet. The Eucharist is also a *sacrifice*. Through the priest, Jesus makes present, in an unbloody manner, the same sacrifice he offered on Calvary for the salvation of the world. In the Eucharistic Celebration, we join in offering Jesus and

also ourselves to the Father. *Eucharist* comes from the Greek word that means "thanksgiving." The Eucharist is the perfect prayer and the source and high point of our Christian life. See *Communion, Holy*.

DID YOU KNOW?

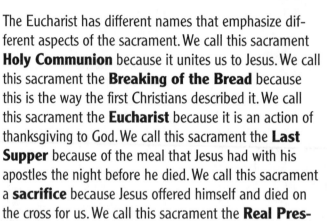

The Eucharist has different names that emphasize different aspects of the sacrament. We call this sacrament **Holy Communion** because it unites us to Jesus. We call this sacrament the **Breaking of the Bread** because this is the way the first Christians described it. We call this sacrament the **Eucharist** because it is an action of thanksgiving to God. We call this sacrament the **Last Supper** because of the meal that Jesus had with his apostles the night before he died. We call this sacrament a **sacrifice** because Jesus offered himself and died on the cross for us. We call this sacrament the **Real Presence** because Jesus is fully present even though we cannot see him. We call this sacrament the **Mass** because it ends by sending us forth so that we may carry out God's will.

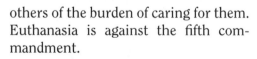

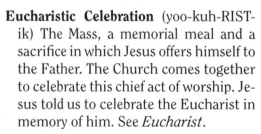

Eucharistic Celebration (yoo-kuh-RIST-ik) The Mass, a memorial meal and a sacrifice in which Jesus offers himself to the Father. The Church comes together to celebrate this chief act of worship. Jesus told us to celebrate the Eucharist in memory of him. See *Eucharist*.

euthanasia (yoo-thuh-NAY-zhuh) So-called mercy killing, or putting someone to death to avoid pain or relieve others of the burden of caring for them. Euthanasia is against the fifth commandment.

evangelical counsels (ee-van-JEL-i-kuhl) Good actions taught and practiced by Christ that lead to perfection. Most men and women religious vow the three evangelical counsels of poverty, chastity, and obedience.

evangelist (i-VAN-juh-list) One of the human writers of the four Gospels: Matthew, Mark, Luke, and John.

DID YOU KNOW?

The four evangelists are often represented by symbols. Matthew the Evangelist is symbolized by a man. This represents the human nature of Christ. Mark the Evangelist is symbolized by a lion. This symbol shows Christ as a king. Luke the Evangelist is symbolized by an ox or bull. These symbols show Christ as a priest. John the Evangelist is symbolized by an eagle. This symbol represents Christ as the all-powerful God.

evangelization (i-VAN-juh-li-zay-shun) Proclaiming to the world by words and actions the saving message of Jesus with the intention of inviting others to be initiated into the Church or to deepen others' faith. Every Christian is called to evangelize.

Eve The first woman. Her name means "mother of all the living," but through the disobedience of Adam and Eve, death entered the world. Our first parents committed the original sin, and all their descendants—with the exception of Jesus and Mary—are born with it. Mary is called the new Eve because, through her cooperation with God, eternal life became possible again.

evil The opposite of good. The term refers to whatever is opposed to God, religion, and morality.

evolution (ev-uh-LOO-shuhn) A process of natural, orderly change through which living things grow from the simple to the more complicated or adapt in other ways to their surroundings. Catholics can believe in evolution as long as they understand that God is the one who began and guides the process and believe that God creates each individual human soul.

examination of conscience (ig-zam-uh-NAY-shuhn of KON-shuhns) The process of reviewing how well one has lived according to the law of God. In an examination of conscience, a person compares his or her thoughts, words, actions, and desires to the way God expects his children to act. Usually a person makes an examination of conscience to prepare for the sacrament of Reconciliation. However, it is a good idea to make it at other times, too—even every day—in order to become a better, more loving person and to grow spiritually.

E

ex cathedra (eks KATH-i-druh) A Latin phrase meaning "from the throne" or "from the chair." When a pope speaks *ex cathedra,* he issues a solemn, infallible statement about faith and morals. The pope speaks as the supreme pastor, using his authority as the successor of Saint Peter, with the intention of obliging the whole Church to believe the teaching. Such a pronouncement by the pope is rare. See *infallibility.*

excommunication (eks-kuh-myoo-ni-KAY-shuhn) The penalty by which a Catholic is cut off from the Church and deprived of the sacraments as a result of committing a very serious offense. Excommunication can be imposed officially by the Church or can occur automatically in the case of certain grave sins.

Exodus (EK-suh-duhs) 1) The great saving event of God leading the Hebrews out of slavery in Egypt to freedom. Moses led them through the Red Sea and into the desert where they wandered for forty years before entering the Promised Land. While in the desert, God gave the Hebrews the commandments and entered into a covenant to make them his chosen people. Jews celebrate the feast of Passover to remember the Exodus. 2) The name of the Bible's second book, which describes the Hebrews' escape from Egypt. See *covenant, Passover.*

exorcism (EK-sor-siz-uhm) Expelling a demon from someone who is possessed by this evil spirit. Jesus had power to cast out devils. Today certain priests, called exorcists, have special permission from the bishop to perform exorcisms. In Baptism, during a prayer of exorcism the priest or deacon prays that the person being baptized be freed from original sin.

exposition of the Blessed Sacrament (ek-spuh-ZISH-uhn) The ritual in which the Eucharist is taken from the tabernacle, placed in a monstrance, and set on the altar for public adoration. Exposition is typically followed by a special blessing with the Eucharist called Benediction. See *Benediction.*

faith (1) One of the theological virtues by which the believer accepts as truth what God has revealed. Through faith, a person believes not because of evidence but because of God's authority. Faith is a gift. (2) For Catholics, the truths found in Scripture and Sacred Tradition and expressed in the creeds and the solemn teachings of the Church.

faithful, the The members of the Catholic Church. They have been baptized in Christ and are joined in faith with the pope.

Fall The original sin of Adam and Eve by which they lost divine friendship and became subject to ignorance, suffering, and death. These consequences of original sin are experienced by the descendants of Adam and Eve.

fast, eucharistic (yoo-kuh-RIST-ik) Eating nothing (water and medicine are permitted) for one hour before receiving Holy Communion in order to prepare to receive Jesus. Fasting helps us focus our minds and hearts on the Eucharist in which Jesus feeds us. The rule of the eucharistic fast does not apply to sick people or to those who are caring for them at the time of the Anointing of the Sick.

fasting Eating and drinking nothing or very little for a religious reason. Fasting is an act of penance by which we unite ourselves to the sufferings of Jesus and help make up for sins. This act of self-denial strengthens our character and also helps us identify with the hungry. On Ash Wednesday and Good Friday, the Church requires adults between the ages of 18 and 60 to limit themselves to only one full meal and two lighter meals that do not equal the main meal. They are not permitted to eat between meals.

Father (1) The name used most often by Jesus to describe the First Person of the Blessed Trinity. Jesus taught us to call God our Father also. (2) The title Catholics use to identify priests because they are leaders in the family of God who offer spiritual support and minister to its members, especially by providing the sacraments.

Fathers of the Church A special title given to outstanding writers and teachers in the early Church who witnessed to the faith. Many of them were also bishops, so this title referred to their authority in the family of God. There were four conditions to merit this title: they must have lived in the early ages of the Church; they must have been known for sanctity of life; they merited the approval of the Church; and they taught true doctrine.

DID YOU KNOW?

Some of the greatest Fathers of the Church were Saint Clement of Rome, Saint Ignatius of Antioch, Saint Polycarp, Saint Ambrose of Milan, Saint Augustine, Saint Jerome, Saint Gregory of Nazianzen, Saint Basil the Great, Saint Gregory of Nyssa, Saint John Chrysostom, and Saint Athanasius.

Fatima, apparitions of (FAT-uh-muh) Visions of the Blessed Virgin Mary that took place in Fatima, Portugal. Preced-

ed by three visits of an angel, Mary appeared to three children—Lucia, Jacinta, and Francisco—six times between May 13 and October 13 of 1917. Mary asked that people pray the Rosary, do penance, and pray and sacrifice for priests and the conversion of sinners. The intention for these good works would be the conversion of Russia and peace. Fatima is now a popular pilgrimage site.

fear of the Lord The gift of the Holy Spirit that means reverence, wonder, and awe in response to God's complete holiness. God knows all, can do all, and is perfect in every way. See *gifts of the Holy Spirit*.

feasts Church celebrations of special events or mysteries that are related to God, Jesus, Mary, or the saints.

first Communion Receiving Jesus in the Holy Eucharist for the first time. This usually takes place after a child has reached the "age of reason," around age seven. Before receiving first Communion, children are to receive the sacrament of Reconciliation, unless they are being baptized the same day.

First Fridays A devotion in honor of the Sacred Heart of Jesus in which Catholics receive Holy Communion on the first Friday of nine months in a row to make up for sins. This practice was requested by Jesus during his apparitions to Saint Margaret Mary Alacoque in the 1600s. Jesus promised that people who carried out this devotion would keep the faith and have a happy death, because they would be consoled by the great love of his Sacred Heart.

fisherman's ring The ring the pope uses to seal important documents. It bears his name and is destroyed when he dies.

font, holy water A cup or bowl-like container at church entrances that holds water that has been blessed. People dip their fingers into the water and make the sign of the cross with  it when they enter or leave the church. This practice is a reminder of Baptism.

forgiveness of sin See *absolution*.

form The words and signs (things and actions) that are necessary for a valid sacrament. For example, in Baptism, certain words must be said and water must be used.

fortitude (FOR-ti-tood) The strength and courage to do what is right even when it is difficult. Fortitude is a gift of the Holy Spirit and a cardinal virtue. See *gifts of the Holy Spirit*.

fortune-telling The superstitious practice of predicting the future through use of crystal balls, tea leaves, cards, and other methods. See *divination*.

Franciscan (fran-SIS-kuhn) A person who vows to follow the Rule of Saint Francis of Assisi, who lived around A.D. 1200. There are Franciscans priests, brothers, and sisters who live in religious congregations. Laypeople can be associated with them  St. Francis and share in their works and prayers by belonging to the Secular Franciscan Order. All Franciscans pledge to imitate Saint Francis, who followed the poor Christ and sought riches in heaven.

frankincense (FRANG-kin-sens) A sweet-smelling resin (dried tree sap) that is burned in religious rites and used in perfumes. One of the Magi brought frankincense to Baby Jesus, a sign of the Savior's priestly role.

free will The ability to make choices without being forced. Free will is a gift from God, one of the ways that we are made in God's likeness. Those who use free will as God intends will be rewarded in eternity. Those who use it to commit sin and who do not repent will be punished.

fruits of the Holy Spirit Virtues and characteristics of those people who are led by the Holy Spirit. *See p. 85 for a list of the fruits.*

fundamentalism (fuhn-duh-MEN-tl-iz-uhm) A literal interpretation of the Scriptures that doesn't take into consideration the historical times and culture of the human authors. Fundamentalists believe that everything in the Bible is a fact. For example, they believe that Methuselah actually lived 969 years. However, scholars who study history and archaeology have learned that the ancient Hebrews would exaggerate the length of a person's life in a story to stress his or her importance. Scholars also know that certain numbers had particular significance to the Hebrews. Fundamentalists often stress being "born again" and the end of the world.

funeral Mass The Mass that is said for a deceased Catholic after a vigil (wake) service and before the procession to the gravesite. The casket is sprinkled with holy water and covered with a white pall as reminders of Baptism. Prayers for the deceased and special readings give hope to those who grieve.

Galilee The northern section of Palestine where Jesus grew up, lived, did most of his teaching, and performed many of his miracles.

Garden of Eden See *Eden, Garden of*.

Gehenna (gi-HEN-uh) (1) A valley near Jerusalem where children were sacrificed to idols. (2) In the New Testament, a fiery place of punishment, hell.

general absolution (ab-suh-LOO-shuhn) A form of the sacrament of Reconciliation that allows a group of people to be forgiven even though they have not made individual confessions. General absolution is only to be given when the people are in danger of death and it would be impossible for a priest to hear all the confessions, or when, due to the insufficient number of priests, a number of people would be deprived of grace and Holy Communion for a long time. Those who receive general absolution must be sorry for their sins and intend to make an individual confession of their mortal sins to a priest as soon as they are able. See *sin, mortal; Reconciliation, sacrament of.*

general intercessions (in-ter-SES-shuns) See *Prayer of the Faithful.*

general judgment See *judgment, general.*

Genesis (JEN-uh-sis) The first book of the Old Testament that tells of the origins of the world, of human beings, and, in particular, of the Jewish people.

genocide (JEN-uh-syd) The crime of killing a great number of innocent people mainly because of their race, tribe, or nation.

Gentile (JEN-tyl) Any person who is not Jewish.

genuflection (jen-yoo-FLEK-shuhn) The reverent practice of bending the right knee to touch the floor. Catholics genuflect before the Blessed Sacrament as a sign of faith and adoration.

Gethsemane (geth-SEM-uh-nee) The garden on the Mount of Olives where Jesus went after the Last Supper and endured his agony. It was in Gethsemane that Jesus was betrayed by Judas and arrested. See *agony of Christ.*

gifts of the Holy Spirit Seven permanent, supernatural dispositions (inclinations) given to us by the Holy Spirit that make it easier to respond to grace and do good. These gifts are given at Baptism and are strengthened in Confirmation. *See p. 85 for a list of these gifts.*

gift of tongues Also called *glossolalia* (glos-uh-LAY-lee-uh), the special ability given by the Holy Spirit to speak a language that is understood by all. It has two forms: (1) Talking in a language that the speaker and the hearers cannot understand. The purpose of this gift is to praise God. (2) Communicating God's message to those who speak a different language. An example of *glossolalia* occurred on Pentecost, when the apostles preached to crowds who spoke many different languages, but the hearers were all able to understand the message.

gifts, supernatural (soo-per-NACH-er-uhl) Blessings that are above human nature and enable those who receive them to live in God's grace. Among these supernatural gifts are the seven gifts of the Holy Spirit and the theological virtues of faith, hope, and love.

glorified body The human body after it has been resurrected from the dead and reunited with its soul at the end of the world. A glorified body is free of all pain and defects and will last forever. It has a wonderful brightness and splendor. It enjoys a spiritual quality that enables it to move from one place to another instantly and to pass through material objects. A glorified body exists in perfect harmony with the soul instead of leading it to sin. Jesus and Mary already have glorified bodies.

gluttony (GLUHT-n-ee) The extreme desire for food or drink or indulging in too much food or drink. Gluttony is a sin against temperance. It is also one of the capital sins. See *sins, capital*.

God The Supreme Being, a pure spirit, who created the universe. God is infinite, almighty, all-knowing, eternal, unchangeable, and perfect in every way. In history, God has revealed himself to us as a Trinity: Father, Son, and Holy Spirit. Because God is so great, human beings can never fully understand or appreciate his perfection. The Bible's definition of God is "God is love" (1 John 4:16).

godparents The persons who act as sponsors for those being baptized. They are expected to encourage and assist their godchildren to learn about and practice the Catholic faith.

Golgotha (GOL-guh-thuh) "Place of the skull"—another name for the hill of Calvary where Jesus was crucified.

Good Friday The day on which Christians remember in a special way the passion and death of Jesus on the Friday before Easter. No Mass is celebrated on this day, but a "Celebration of the Lord's Passion" is held, which includes the reading of the Passion from John's Gospel, intercessions, veneration of the cross, and Holy Communion.

Good Shepherd A title that Jesus used to describe himself (John 10:11–18). Just as a shepherd knows each of his sheep and protects them all—even giving up his own life to keep them safe—so Jesus knows and cares for each of us, his

followers, and has laid down his life for our salvation. Psalm 23 is known as the Good Shepherd psalm.

Gospel (1) The Good News that the Savior promised in the Old Testament has come and the whole message of faith he revealed. The word *gospel* is derived from an Old English term for "good news." (2) In the New Testament, the four accounts of the life, teaching, and saving work of Jesus written by Matthew, Mark, Luke, and John.

grace The gift of God's life within the human soul. Through grace, we receive help from God to achieve salvation. No one has a right to grace. Instead, it is a purely generous gift from God, who is all good.

grace, actual The assistance God offers us during our earthly life to enable us to perform good actions. Actual grace helps us to understand holy things and makes us stronger in avoiding sin and in choosing what is right.

grace at meals Prayers said before and after eating, to thank God for his gifts and to ask his blessing.

grace, sanctifying (SANK-tuh-fy-ing) The lasting presence of God in us that makes us holy, more like him. Sanctifying grace is first received at Baptism. Sin drives it away.

greed See *avarice*.

Guadalupe, Our Lady of (gwad-ah-LOO-pay) The title given to Mary, the Mother of God, after she appeared to Juan Diego in Mexico in December 1531. Mary asked that a church be built at the site. To convince the bishop of her appearance, Mary had Juan Diego pick roses in December on a barren hill and

printed a permanent picture of herself on his cloak. Our Lady of Guadalupe, whose feast is celebrated on December 12, is the patroness of all the Americas.

guardian angels (GAHR-dee-uhn) Spiritual beings God appoints to assist human beings. Guardian angels pray for us, help us become holier, protect us from spiritual and physical dangers, and present our prayers to God. Jesus referred to them in Matthew 18:10. See *angels*.

guilt (1) The condition of a person responsible for doing evil and who faces punishment. (2) The negative feeling a person has after committing sin.

habit, religious The uniforms of sisters, brothers, and priests that identify them as a member of a particular religious order or congregation. Religious wear the habit as a sign of their dedication to God and to the Church.

habitual grace (huh-BICH-oo-uhl) See *grace, sanctifying*.

Hail Mary The most familiar prayer in honor of Mary, the Mother of God. The first sentence of the Hail Mary is the angel Gabriel's greeting at the annunciation. The second sentence is composed of the words Elizabeth spoke when Mary arrived to visit her. The name *Jesus* was added to identify the fruit of Mary's womb. The last sentence is a petition for Mary's prayers "now and at the hour of our death."

hair shirt A rough, uncomfortable shirt usually made of animal hair and worn as an act of penance and mortification (discipline of the will) long ago when ideas of spirituality were different from our own today.

halo (HAY-loh) A disk or circle of light that symbolizes the holiness of God and in art appears around the head of Jesus, a saint, or an angel.

Hanukkah (HAH-nuh-kuh), also spelled Chanukah (KHAH-nuh-kuh) An eight-day Jewish celebration of the re-dedication of the Temple of Jerusalem in 165 B.C. The Jews had won victory over the Syrians, who had sacrificed pigs to Zeus in the Temple. Hanukkah is also called Feast of Lights and centers on lighting the candles of the menorah (an eight-branched candleholder).

hatred Extreme dislike of something or someone. Jesus calls his followers to love one another, and so it is wrong to hate anyone. It's certainly all right to hate sin, but it's wrong to hate the sinner.

heaven (HEV-uhn) Where God dwells, the state of unending and complete happiness that is the destiny God plans for us.

hell A state of complete and unending separation from God and therefore of misery and real suffering. The fallen angels were condemned to hell because of their sin. Persons who die in the state of mortal sin, freely refusing God's love and mercy, also go to hell. Jesus spoke of the fires of hell, but we don't know all the details about hell. We do know that those in hell will suffer a great deal and that hell is final.

heresy (HER-uh-see) A religious teaching that is in opposition to a Church doctrine revealed by God. See *doctrine*.

heretic (HER-i-tik) A person who commits heresy.

hermit A person who lives all alone so that he or she can grow closer to God through prayer, silence, and sacrifice.

heroic virtue (hi-ROH-ik) The extraordinary practice of faith, hope, and charity, along with the cardinal virtues. The practice of heroic virtue is a requirement for a person to be canonized. See *canonization*.

hierarchy (HY-er-ar-key) The clergy: the pope, bishops, priests, and deacons, who receive the sacrament of Holy Orders. They carry on Christ's work and serve the members of the Church by teaching, governing, and sanctifying them. See *Holy Orders*.

high priest A civil and religious leader at the time of Jesus, the high priest presided over the Sanhedrin (Jewish council) and great ceremonies. He was the only one permitted to enter the holy of holies in the Temple and only on the Day of Atonement so that he could make offerings for the people. The Letter to the Hebrews calls Jesus Christ a high priest because he offers himself in reparation for the sins of all people.

holiness (1) Closeness to God; sanctity; goodness; sharing the life of God. Everyone is called to holiness and can attain it through God's grace, the help of the Holy Spirit, and prayer. (2) One of the four identifying characteristics, or marks, of the Catholic Church. The Church is holy because it was founded by Christ, shares in the holy mission of Jesus, is guided by the Holy Spirit, teaches holy doctrines, and gives members the assistance they need to live holy lives.

holy Sacred; belonging to God, the all-holy One. If an object or place is blessed, it is called "holy."

Holy Communion See *Communion, Holy*.

holy days of obligation (ob-li-GAY-shuhn) Important feast days in the Church calendar that Catholics are required to celebrate by participating in Mass and avoiding the performance of hard work. A country's bishops may remove the obligation or move the celebration to a Sunday. *See p. 83 for the list of holy days.*

Holy Family Jesus, Mary, and Joseph make up the Holy Family, which is a model for all Christian families.

Holy Father A title for the pope, who is the spiritual father of all who believe in Christ.

holy hour An hour of prayer spent in the presence of Jesus in the Blessed Sacrament. The practice is an act of faith in the Real Presence of Christ in the Eucharist. A holy hour often includes reflection on the passion of the Savior. During his suffering in Gethsemane, Jesus asked: "So, could you not stay awake with me one hour? Stay awake and pray..." (Matthew 26:40–41). In making a holy hour, believers follow this advice of Jesus. See *Real Presence, Eucharist*.

holy of holies The most sacred part of the Temple where the ark of the covenant was kept until it disappeared. Only the high priest could enter the room and only once a year on the Day of Atonement.

Holy Land Israel; Palestine; Canaan. This was the land that God promised Abraham and his descendants, and where Jesus was born and lived. Israel has three provinces: Galilee in the north, Judah in the south, and Samaria between them.

PALESTINE AT THE TIME OF CHRIST

holy oils See *oils, holy*.

Holy Orders The sacrament through which a man is ordained and given the grace and power to serve Christ and his Church, especially by administering the sacraments of the Eucharist, Reconciliation, Baptism, and so on. Holy Orders has three degrees: deacon, priest, and bishop (the highest). Only a bishop can administer this sacrament, which is accomplished through the laying on of hands and the  words of the consecrating prayer. Jesus instituted (which means he established) this sacrament on Holy Thursday.

Holy Saturday The day before Easter when the Church remembers how the body of Jesus lay in the tomb awaiting his glorious resurrection.

Holy See (1) The place where the pope lives and where the central offices of the Church are located in Vatican City. (2) The pope, along with the Roman Curia (congregations, councils, and departments) that assist him as well as the delegates to and from many nations. (3) The authority of the Holy Father as teacher and leader of the Church.

holy souls The souls in purgatory, who are saved but must first be purified and perfected in love before entering the presence of God in heaven. We can pray for them. See *purgatory*.

Holy Spirit The Third Person of the Blessed Trinity, who is equal to the Father and the Son. Through the power of the Holy Spirit, God became man. The Spirit was sent to guide the Church and make its members holy on Pentecost. Other names for the Holy Spirit are Counselor, Paraclete (Advocate), the Sanctifier, and Finger of God's Right Hand.

DID YOU KNOW?

The Holy Spirit is often pictured as a dove. This symbolism is taken directly from the Bible. In Matthew 3:16, we read: "And when Jesus had been baptized, just as he came up from the water, suddenly the heavens were opened to him and he saw the Spirit of God descending like a dove and alighting on him."

Holy Thursday The Thursday in Holy Week, during which Christians remember the Last Supper, Jesus' agony in the Garden of Gethsemane, and his arrest and torture by the Roman soldiers. On

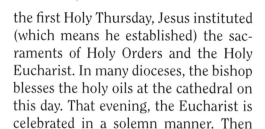

the first Holy Thursday, Jesus instituted (which means he established) the sacraments of Holy Orders and the Holy Eucharist. In many dioceses, the bishop blesses the holy oils at the cathedral on this day. That evening, the Eucharist is celebrated in a solemn manner. Then the altar is stripped and the Blessed Sacrament is taken to another place for solemn adoration until midnight.

holy water Water blessed by priests or deacons and used as a sacramental in making other things holy. For example, homes, cars, and other items are often sprinkled with holy water when they are blessed. Holy water is also used in Baptism. During certain other liturgical celebrations, the priest sprinkles the people with holy water.

holy water font See *font, holy water*.

Holy Week The sacred week during which the Church solemnly remembers the last days of Jesus' earthly life. Holy Week begins with Passion (Palm) Sunday and ends with Holy Saturday.

homily (HOM-uh-lee) The preaching that follows the Gospel at Mass. In the homily, the priest (or deacon) explains the Scriptures.

homosexuality (hoh-muh-sek-shoo-AL-i-tee) (1) Same-sex attraction; not sinful in itself. (2) Sexual activity between persons of the same sex. These acts are sinful because these unions are not according to God's plan for marriage and family life.

hope The theological virtue that enables a person to trust in the saving help of God, who wants all people to reach heaven. Through hope, a person is confident that God will keep his promises and turn sorrow into joy.

hosanna (hoh-ZAN-uh) The Hebrew word *hosanna*, which means "save us, we pray!" was used as a joyful greeting when Jesus entered Jerusalem before the Passover. We repeat it and wave palms on Passion Sunday. In every Mass, *hosanna* is included in the jubilant hymn "Holy, Holy, Holy" at the beginning of the eucharistic prayer before Jesus comes to us.

host (1) A victim offered to God in sacrifice. Jesus is the spotless Host offered to the Father at the Last Supper, on Calvary, and at every Mass. (2) The host is also the bread that is consecrated during the Mass and becomes Jesus.

human soul See *soul, human*.

humility (hyoo-MIL-i-tee) The virtue through which people have a truthful understanding of their relationship with God and an awareness that all the good they possess comes from him.

hymn (him) A holy song addressed to God or the saints or about a religious mystery and usually sung in worship.

icon (EYE-kon) Religious art of the Eastern Church in which pictures of Jesus, Mary, the angels, or the saints are painted on a wall or wood or metal and covered with silver or gold. The colors and figures are symbolic. The painter prays and  fasts while painting. For Eastern Christians, the icon is a window into heaven and very sacred.

idol (EYE-dol) A false god; any picture, statue, or other object that is worshiped as though it were almighty God.

idolatry (eye-DOL-uh-tree) The act of worshiping a false god and therefore a sin against the first commandment.

IHS The first three letters of the Greek word for "Jesus." These letters often appear on holy objects such as altars and hosts.

image and likeness of God Similarity to God. Human beings were created to be like God in that they have a spiritual nature and an immortal soul, endowed with a mind and free will.

Immaculate Conception (i-MAK-yuh-lit kuhn-SEP-shuhn) Mary's preservation from original sin from the moment she was conceived. Mary received this unique privilege because she was to be the Mother of Jesus. Because Jesus is all holy, it was right that Mary be preserved from sin. The Immaculate Conception was proclaimed a dogma in 1854. We celebrate the feast of the Immaculate Conception on December 8. It is a holy day of obligation in the United States.

immersion, Baptism by (i-MUR-zhuhn) A method of celebrating the sacrament of Baptism in which a person goes completely under water three times while the words of Baptism are said. Immersion symbolizes going down with Jesus into death and then rising again to a new life of grace.

immortality (im-or-TAL-i-tee) The quality

of living forever. Human beings' spiritual souls will one day be united with their bodies and they will live forever. Jesus promised us eternal life.

immutability (i-MYOO-tuh-bil-i-tee) God's unchangeableness. Because God is perfect and spiritual, he does not need to improve and is not affected by the physical changes we experience.

impeccability (im-PEK-uh-bil-i-tee) The inability to sin. Because Jesus is the Son of God and therefore divine, he enjoyed impeccability during his earthly life. Once people die and go to heaven, they are also impeccable. After someone has experienced the beatific vision, it is then impossible for him or her to sin. See *beatific vision*.

imprimatur (im-pri-MAH-ter) Approval that a bishop gives to indicate that a book dealing with faith or morals is in keeping with Catholic doctrine. *Imprimatur* is the Latin word for "let it be printed."

Incarnation (in-kahr-NAY-shuhn) The union of the divinity of the Second Person of the Blessed Trinity with humanity in the person of Jesus Christ. Because Jesus is the Son of God, he is divine. Because he is the Son of Mary, he is human. Jesus is one divine Person with two natures, one divine and one human. This doctrine is at the center of Catholic belief.

incense Resin, from plants and trees, sprinkled on glowing coals at liturgies to produce fragrant smoke. The smoke symbolizes our prayers of adoration rising to heaven. The altar, ministers, and congregation may be incensed.

indulgence (in-DUHL-juhns) The canceling (or lessening) of the punishment for sin that is to be undergone on earth or in purgatory. The Church grants indulgences for various good actions and prayers. Indulgences can be earned for oneself or for the holy souls in purgatory.

infallibility (in-FAL-uh-bil-i-tee) The inability to make a mistake when teaching about faith or morals. The Holy Spirit's guidance and protection gives the Church this gift. Because of it, the Church as a whole remains faithful to the message of Jesus. The pope, too, is infallible when he speaks to the whole Church and teaches *ex cathedra*. The worldwide college of bishops is also infallible when it joins with the Holy Father in deciding that a doctrine is to be held by all the faithful. The pope is the one who actually proclaims such a teaching. See *ex cathedra*.

infinite (IN-fuh-nit) This term refers to God's limitlessness. Because God is infinite and we are finite (limited), we are not able to fully understand God.

infusion, Baptism by (in-FYOO-zhuhn) The method of Baptism by which water is poured on a person being baptized. Usually the water is poured in the form of a cross over the head of the person being baptized while the minister of Baptism says the words.

I.N.R.I. Initials that Pontius Pilate ordered placed on the cross of Christ to indicate his crime. They stood for the Latin words that mean "Jesus of Nazareth, King of the Jews."

inspiration (in-spuh-RAY-shun) The influence that God exerted over the human writers of Scripture so that he acted in them and by them, but they remained genuine authors. They used their own style and skills but wrote exactly what God wanted and no more.

intercession (in-ter-SESH-uhn) A type of prayer in which one asks for God's blessings for others. We can offer prayers of intercession for both the living and the dead. Mary and the saints can intercede for us.

Israel (1) The name given to Jacob after he fought with an angel. See Genesis 32:28. (2) The name of the Hebrew nation populated by Jacob's descendants; the Holy Land.

Jerusalem (ji-ROO-suh-luhm) The city in southern Israel that King David made the capital. It is the Holy City and the City of David. Here the Temple was built and rebuilt, and here Jesus died. Today three major religious groups—Jews, Christians, and Muslims—look upon sites in Jerusalem as holy places.

Jesuits (JEZ-oo-its) A religious order of men known as the Society of Jesus founded in 1540 by

St. Ignatius was the founder of the Jesuits.

Saint Ignatius of Loyola. Jesuits now serve God's people in 112 nations and are one of the largest religious orders in the Catholic Church.

Jesus The name of the Savior, the Son of God, which means "God saves" in Hebrew. God told Mary and Joseph to give him this name. See *Christ*.

Jesus Prayer An ancient prayer that is repeated over and over and leads to contemplation: "Lord Jesus Christ, Son of David, have mercy on me, a sinner." It is based on the story of a blind beggar on the roadside who cried out as Jesus passed, "Jesus, Son of David, have mercy on me!" (Mark 10:47). Saying the Jesus Prayer is a way to draw closer to Jesus, our loving and powerful friend.

Jews (1) Those who profess the religion of Judaism. (2) The people descended from Jacob who followed the Mosaic religion. They were named for their country, Judah.

John the Baptist The relative of Jesus who prepared his way by preaching repentance. His mother was Elizabeth and his father was Zechariah. John baptized Jesus in the Jordan River  and was beheaded for his preaching.

Joseph The husband of Mary and the legal father of Jesus. Joseph was not the nat-  ural father of Jesus, who was conceived in Mary by the power of the Holy Spirit. God chose Saint Joseph, a carpenter, to take care of the Mother of God and of the young Jesus. Saint Joseph is the patron saint of workers, of the universal Church, and of the dying.

joy The fruit of the Holy Spirit that is the special happiness believers possess. Joy is not the same as pleasure, which is physical and easily comes and goes. True Christian joy is the deep, inner happi- ness that comes from knowing that God loves us and is faithful to his promises. God has given us many blessings and has many more in store for those who love him.

jubilee (JOO-buh-lee) In the Book of Leviticus, a celebration that took place every fiftieth year in which lands would be returned to their rightful owners. Jubilee was a special year of forgiveness and joy. Since at least the fourteenth century, the Church has celebrated a jubilee. Today the Catholic jubilee celebration, also called the "Holy Year," occurs every twenty-five years. During this year, special graces are attached to pilgrimages made to local cathedrals or to Saint Peter's in Rome.

Judah (JOO-duh) (1) One of Jacob's twelve sons from whose tribe the Messiah came. (2) The southern province of Israel.

Judaism (JOO-duh-ism) The religious beliefs and practices of the Jewish people, who profess faith in the one true God. The foundation of Judaism is the Old Testament covenant between Yahweh (God) and his people (the Jews).

The star of David is a symbol of Judaism.

judgment, general (JUHJ-muhnt) The judging and sentencing that will take place at the end of the world. At that time, Jesus will come again to judge all people who have ever lived. All those who have died will rise from their

47

graves. The bodies of those who are saved will be glorious, while the bodies of those who are condemned to hell will suffer the punishment they deserve. In Matthew 25:31–45, Jesus describes the judgment as being based on the corporal works of mercy. See *corporal works of mercy*.

judgment, particular The judgment before God that takes place right after a person dies. The soul of the person will

then go to heaven, purgatory, or hell, depending on the free choices the person made in his or her life.

justice (JUHS-tis) (1) The cardinal virtue that enables us to give to God and others what is due them. (2) Righteousness, holiness.

justification (juhs-tuh-fi-KAY-shun) God's action by which we are freed from sins and made holy by grace.

kingdom of God God's reign of peace, justice, mercy, and love that Jesus taught about and came to establish. We pray for its coming in the Our Father and work to bring it about. The Church is the seed of this kingdom, which will come to fulfillment in eternity.

knowledge (NOL-ij) The gift of the Holy Spirit that enables us to know God and what he expects of us. Knowledge helps us find the correct path to heaven. See *gifts of the Holy Spirit*.

laity (LAY-i-tee) The faithful accepted into the Church through Baptism. The laity does not include those who have received Holy Orders and those who have been consecrated as religious. See *Holy Orders, religious life*.

Lamb of God A title for Jesus used by John the Baptist in John 1:36 to identify him. It is also found in the Book of Rev-  elation. The Jews sacrificed lambs as a religious rite. In addition, in the Exodus story, the blood of a lamb marked the doors of Hebrew houses and saved them from death in Egypt. Similarly, the blood of Jesus shed on the cross saved the human race. We address Jesus as Lamb of God at Mass as the priest breaks the consecrated host shortly before Communion.

La Salette, Our Lady of (LAH sa-LET) The name given to Our Lady after she appeared to two children, Maximin Giraud and Melanie Mathieu, in La Sal-ette, France, in 1846. Mary was weeping, and her message was to pray and do penance because her Son was angry at the people's sins. Today there is a large church at the site.

last judgment See *judgment, general*.

last sacraments The sacraments of Reconciliation, Holy Eucharist, and the Anointing of the Sick when they are given to those who are dying. The sacrament of Confirmation may also be given to a gravely ill person if he or she has not yet received it. Each of these sacraments gives the sick person the grace needed to prepare well for death and for passage into eternity. It is important to call a priest to give these sacraments to the dying so their sins can be forgiven and they can be comforted and helped by Jesus.

Last Supper The meal that Jesus shared with his apostles in Jerusalem on Holy Thursday, the day before he was put to death. At the Last Supper, which perhaps was the Passover meal, Jesus instituted the sacraments of the Holy Eucharist and of Holy Orders. He also spoke about

J
K
L

his relationship with his Father. By washing the feet of his apostles, Jesus showed them that those who lead must be humble and love those they serve. See *Eucharist, Holy Orders*.

law In general, law is a rule about what we should or should not do, based on reason and directed to the common good. God's law tells us how to act virtuously and avoid sin. The Church has rules to govern itself, found in canon law. Civil law concerns the laws that society makes for its citizens.

law, canon See Code of Canon Law.

lectio divina (LEX-ee-oh di-VEE-nah) A way of praying with Scripture that originated with communities of monks and nuns and is popular today. It has four steps: reading a passage, reflecting on it, responding with the heart, and resting in God's presence. See *monk, nun*.

lectionary (LEK-shuh-ner-ee) The official book that contains the Scripture readings used during the Liturgy of the Word at Mass.

lector A person who proclaims the Scripture readings during the Mass.

Lent The forty-day liturgical season extending from Ash Wednesday to Holy Thursday when believers prepare for the celebration of Easter. They pray, do penance, and help the poor. By spending this time well, Christians can grow in faith and change their lives for the better.

levitation (lev-i-TAY-shuhn) The phenomenon in which a person is raised above the ground with no support. Some saints had the gift of levitation.

limbo (LIM-boh) The home of natural happiness that theologians proposed for two groups of deceased people unable to enter heaven: (1) the holy people who died before the time of Jesus and who had to wait until he opened the gates of heaven through his death and resurrection; and (2) unbaptized infants. Limbo is not an official Church teaching. We do not know how God deals with unbaptized infants, but we have reason to hope that God will bring them to salvation.

litany (LIT-n-ee) A prayer composed of a list of names or titles followed by a response that is repeated many times. For example, in the Litany of the Saints, after each saint's name is said, the response is "pray for us." Other litanies are the Litany of Loreto, which is a Marian prayer, and the Litany of the Sacred Heart.

liturgical year (li-TUR-ji-kuhl) The feasts and seasons that span an entire year in the Church's celebration of Jesus' life, death, and resurrection. The liturgical year, also called the Church year, is divided into five seasons: Advent, Christmas, Lent, Easter, and Ordinary Time. It begins on the First Sunday of Advent and ends with the celebration of Christ the King.

DID YOU KNOW?

During the liturgical year, the bishop or priest wears vestments of different liturgical colors at Mass. The colors relate to the particular season or feast being celebrated. Green, which symbolizes life and hope, is used during Ordinary Time. Purple symbolizes penance and is used during Advent and Lent. It may also be used on All Souls' Day and at Masses for the Dead. White symbolizes purity and triumph. It is used during the Christmas and Easter seasons, feasts of Jesus and Mary, Holy Thursday, feasts of angels and non-martyred saints, at weddings, and also at funerals. Red stands for blood and fire. It is used on Pentecost, Palm Sunday, Good Friday, feasts of the Holy Cross and the martyrs, and Masses in honor of the Holy Spirit.

liturgy (LIT-er-jee) The Church's official public worship, including the celebration of Mass, the sacraments, and the Liturgy of the Hours. During the liturgy, the priest acts for Christ and makes his grace present by the power of the Holy Spirit.

Liturgy of the Hours The official prayer of the Church, also called the Divine Office, which priests and religious pray every day. All the faithful are encouraged to pray it as well. It consists mostly of scriptural prayers prayed at different hours during the day, making the entire day holy.

Liturgy of the Word That part of the Mass in which we listen to and reflect upon Sacred Scripture.

Liturgy of the Eucharist (YOO-kuh-rist) That part of the Mass following the Liturgy of the Word when Jesus offers himself and we offer ourselves together with him to the Father. In the Liturgy of the Eucharist, our gifts of bread and wine become the Body and Blood of Jesus Christ, whom we receive in Holy Communion.

Lord The name we use for God the Father and his Son, Jesus. Out of reverence, the chosen people did not say or read aloud the holy, personal name of God revealed to Moses, which was YHWH. They used the word *Adonai,* a Hebrew word that means "Lord." When vowels were added to YHWH, the name became Yahweh and also Jehovah.

Lord's Day See *Sabbath*.

Lord's Prayer A prayer composed of seven petitions that Jesus himself taught to his followers. It is a summary of the Gospel. Catholics commonly call this prayer the Our Father, taking the title from its opening words. The early Christians prayed the Lord's Prayer three times a day. Today we pray it during every Mass. People preparing to join the Church recite the Our Father along with the Creed in a special rite.

Lourdes, Our Lady of (loordz) Title given to Mary after she appeared, beginning on February 11, 1858, to fourteen-year-old Bernadette Soubirous in Lourdes, France. Mary identified herself as the Immaculate Conception, a doctrine that had just been defined by the Church in

St. Bernadette Soubirous

1854. At Mary's request, a church was built on the site. Lourdes is now a popular place where pilgrims go hoping for graces or even bodily healing. So far, the Church has approved sixty-seven miracles that have taken place at the Lourdes shrine. See *miracle*.

love See *charity*.

lust A disordered desire for earthly pleasures, especially sexual pleasures. Lust is a capital sin. See *sins, capital*.

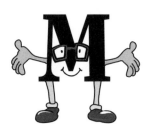

Madonna (muh-DON-uh) A title for Mary, the Mother of Jesus, which is related to the Latin and Italian words meaning "my lady."

Magi (MAY-jeye) The wise men who came from the East to visit Jesus soon after his birth. They were led on their journey by a star, and they honored Jesus as the newborn King of the Jews. Because they gave him three gifts of gold, frankincense, and myrrh, it is commonly held

that there were three wise men. Many believe the Magi were kings. Their visit shows that Jesus had come not only for his own people, the Jews, but also for all people of the world. Jesus is the King of kings.

magisterium (maj-uh-STEER-ee-uhm) The official teaching authority of the Church used in explaining and preserving the Church teachings found in the Bible and Sacred Tradition. Jesus gave the pope and the bishops in communion with him this authority, and the Holy Spirit was sent to guide the Church always. The role of the magisterium is to make sure that we, God's people, always live in the truth that makes us free. See *Tradition, Sacred*.

Magnificat (mag-NIF-i-kaht) The Latin name for Mary's joyful response to Elizabeth's greeting. After the annunciation, Mary had gone to help this older relative during her pregnancy. This canticle is found in Luke 1:46–55 and is recited or sung daily in the Liturgy of the Hours.

manna (MAN-uh) The bread from heaven that God sent to the Israelites while they wandered in the desert for forty years after escaping from slavery in Egypt. Manna was small, round, white flakes found on the ground. It tasted like wafers made with honey. This miraculous food is considered a symbol of the Holy Eucharist, which is our food for the journey of life.

marks of the Church The four most important characteristics or qualities of the Catholic Church one, holy, catholic (universal), and apostolic. Originally meant to be ideals for the Church, these marks became seen as ways to identify the Catholic Church as Christ's true Church. They are listed in the Nicene Creed.

martyr (MAR-ter) A person who willingly gives up his or her life for the sake of the faith. A martyr refuses to deny Jesus and his teachings, even if this act of courage means suffering and death. The Church has declared many martyrs to be saints.

Mary, Blessed Virgin (BLES-id VUR-jin) The Mother of Jesus, and therefore the Mother of God. The Council of Ephesus in 431 gave the title *Theotokos* (a Greek word meaning "God-bearer") to Mary. Chosen by God, Mary became the Mother of Jesus through the power of the Holy Spirit and cooperated with her Son in the salvation of the world. Mary was preserved from all sin, even original sin, and was the perfect disciple of Jesus. She accompanied him to Calvary, where from the cross Jesus gave her to us as our mother. With the apostles, Mary was present at Pentecost when the Holy Spirit came. She is the Mother of the Church. At the end of her life, Mary was assumed body and soul into heaven, where she reigns as Queen of Heaven and Earth and intercedes for us.

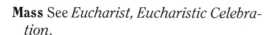

Mass See *Eucharist, Eucharistic Celebration*.

Matrimony (MA-truh-moh-nee) Marriage, the sacrament in which a baptized man and woman are married. They make a covenant, vowing to be committed to each other in a lifelong union, to share an exclusive love, and to

A symbol of matrimony.

be open to bringing children into the world. The sacrament usually occurs within a Mass, which is called a nuptial Mass.

mediator (MEE-dee-ay-ter) A title of Jesus, who reconciled the human race and God. A mediator is one who "stands in the middle" and speaks or acts on behalf of someone else. The sin of our first parents broke the relationship between God and the human race. But Jesus, the God-Man, atoned for this sin, making it possible for us once again to possess grace and enjoy friendship with God.

meditation (med-i-TAY-shuhn) A form of mental prayer in which a person thinks about God and the things of God in order to grow closer to him.

meekness (MEEK-ness) A virtue and one of the fruits of the Holy Spirit that helps one to moderate anger and to deal with troubles calmly and even with a sense of humor.

Memorare (mem-uh-RAH-ray) A well-loved prayer composed by Saint Bernard of Clairvaux in the twelfth century in which we address Mary and ask for her help and protection. It takes its name from its first word, "remember," in Latin.

St. Bernard

mental reservation (MEN-tl rez-er-VAY-shuhn) The act of providing information in a way that limits the sense of the speaker's words to a certain meaning. This is permitted in certain circumstances when one is bound in conscience not to tell the entire truth, for example, to protect confidential information. But it is never permitted to directly tell a lie.

mercy (MUR-see) Compassion, forgiveness, extending help to the needy. The mercy of God is limitless.

merit (MER-it) The "right" to a reward offered by God to those who obey his commands. No human being can actually have a strict "right" to heaven, but God *freely rewards* his faithful children who cooperate with their God-given graces.

Messiah (mi-SY-uh) Refers to Christ, the "anointed one." The prophets told the people he was coming. The Jewish people waited many centuries for his arrival. When he did come, many did not recognize him because they expected the Messiah to be a king or other powerful ruler. Instead, Jesus came in humility. He taught us about the kingdom of God, where riches and power count for nothing and where love and service make a person great in God's eyes.

ministry (MIN-uh-stree) Service related to the mission of the Church. For example, bishops, priests, and deacons share an ordained ministry of administering the sacraments to the faithful. Laypeople have other ministries of service. For example, a catechist has the ministry of teaching the faith, while a lector has the ministry of proclaiming the Word of God at Mass. All are called to serve God and his Church with generosity and dedication. See *bishop, priest, deacon.*

miracle (MIR-uh-kuhl) An action or event during which the laws of nature are suspended. Miracles are often called "signs" or "wonders." Only God can perform miracles. Jesus worked many miracles during his life on earth. He healed lepers and restored sight to the blind. He multiplied a few loaves and fishes to feed thousands of people. He even walked on the water. The greatest miracle was Christ's resurrection. When saints perform miracles, God is actually working these wonders through them.

Miraculous Medal (mi-RAK-yuh-luhs MED-ul) An oval metal disk that shows Mary surrounded by the words, "O Mary conceived without sin, pray for us who have recourse to thee," on one side. On the reverse side, there is the letter M

with a cross above it and the hearts of Jesus and Mary under it, all encircled by twelve stars. In 1830, Our Lady appeared to Saint Catherine Labouré when she was a young sister in Paris and asked that the medal be made and worn around the neck as a sign of love for Mary and trust in her help.

missionaries (MISH-uh-ner-eez) Those people who, like the apostles, tell others about Jesus and the Gospel he preached and continue his work. Often they travel to distant, unfamiliar places, but they may also minister in their own country as home missionaries. Among other things, Catholic missionaries serve in parishes, schools, hospitals, and orphanages. They are in every part of the world.

miter (MY-ter) The tall, pointed headdress worn by bishops and abbots during liturgical services.

modesty (MOD-uh-stee) A virtue that helps us to exercise self-control in speech, dress, and behavior—especially in regard to sexuality. Someone who is modest doesn't tempt others to sinful sexual behavior. Modesty is a fruit of the Holy Spirit.

monastery (MON-uh-ster-ee) The place where a group of monks or nuns live. Usually a monastery is "cloistered." That means that people who do not belong to the religious community cannot enter certain areas.

monk A man who takes vows of poverty, chastity, and obedience and lives in a monastery with other monks. There, apart from the rest of the world, he prays and performs penance. He does these things in order to grow closer to God.

monsignor (mon-SEE-nyer) A title of honor granted by the pope to certain priests.

monstrance (MON-struhns) The sacred vessel that holds the Blessed Sacrament when it is displayed for public adoration or Benediction. Through the clear glass container—called a *luna*—in the center,  we can see the consecrated Host. Usually the monstrance has rays surrounding the center to symbolize the many graces that come to us from the Holy Eucharist. The monstrance is often placed on the altar. At times, it is carried in a procession.

morality (muh-RAL-i-tee) The goodness or badness of human actions. Because we are free, we can choose to do what is right or wrong. God has given us guidelines: the Ten Commandments, the teachings of the Gospel, and the laws of the Church. When we choose to do what is right, we please God. When we choose what is evil, we commit sin and lose grace. Knowing what is moral (right) and what is immoral (wrong) is very important.

Morning Offering (MOR-ning AW-fer-ing) A prayer said at the beginning of the day. Those who pray the Morning Offering join their lives to the offering of Jesus himself for the salvation of the world.

mortal sin See *sin, mortal*.

mortification (mor-tuh-fi-KAY-shuhn) The practice of doing something difficult or sacrificing something for the love of God. Acts of mortification help us to grow in self-control so that we more easily resist sin and practice virtue. Giving up candy in Lent is an example of mortification.

mysteries of the Rosary (ROH-zuh-ree) Twenty events in the life of Jesus and Mary on which we meditate while praying with rosary beads. *See p. 85 for a list of these mysteries.*

mystery (MIS-tuh-ree) A truth that is too deep for human beings to fully understand. God is a mystery that we will never understand. While we can't understand the mysteries of our faith completely, we believe because God has revealed them to us.

mystic (MIS-tik) A person with special spiritual gifts received through contemplation and meditation.

Mystical Body of Christ See *Body of Christ*.

Nativity (nuh-TIV-i-tee) The birth of Jesus in Bethlehem. We celebrate this event on Christmas Day, December 25. It is a holy day of obligation. The Church also remembers two other important birth dates. There are liturgical celebrations for the nativity of Mary (September 8) and of Saint John the Baptist (June 24).

natural family planning A way of spacing out births that uses *natural* ways of identifying fertile and infertile times. Fertile refers to those times when a woman is physically capable of conceiving a child.

natural law (NACH-er-uhl) The code of what is right and wrong that God put in the heart of every human being.

nature (NAY-cher) The essence or substance of a being that gives rise to its characteristics and what it does.

Nazarene (NAZ-uh-reen) or Nazorean (naz-OR-ee-an) Someone who comes from Nazareth in Galilee. Jesus was called by this name because he grew up and lived in that small village until beginning his public ministry.

New Testament (noo TEST-a-ment) The twenty-seven books of the Bible, also known as the Christian Scriptures, that tell of the new covenant. The New Testament includes the four Gospels, the Acts of the Apostles, letters or epistles to the early churches, and the Book of Revelation. *See p. 87 for a list of the New Testament books.*

Nicene Creed (NY-seen creed) The profession of faith that we say during Mass. It came from the teachings of the councils of Nicaea and First Constantinople in the fourth century.

novena (noh-VEE-nuh) A prayer said for nine days or once a week for nine weeks. *Novem* is Latin for "nine." The practice is based on the nine days that Mary and the apostles prayed before the coming of the Holy Spirit on Pentecost.

novice (NOV-is) A person who is in the beginning formation stage of religious life. This stage of prayer and study of the congregation is called the novitiate.

nun (1) Strictly speaking, a woman who has made solemn vows and who lives a cloistered, contemplative life in a monastery. Like a monk, she lives apart from the rest of the world and is devoted to a life of prayer and penance. (2) Commonly used to refer to any woman religious as a synonym for *sister*.

nuptial Mass (NUHP-shuhl) A Mass during which a couple celebrates the sacrament of Matrimony.

O-antiphons (oh-AN-tu-fons) The prayers prayed on the seven days before Christmas that each begin with O and call on Christ by a certain title. They are prayed at evening prayer and form the verses of the Advent song "O Come, O Come, Emmanuel."

oath A calling upon God to witness to the truthfulness of what one says.

oblates (OH-blaytz) Lay persons who have dedicated themselves to God and to living poor, chaste, and obedient lives. Oblates are associated with a particular religious order.

occasion of sin (oh-KAY-zhuhn) A person, place, or thing that often or always tempts one to sin. A person is obliged to avoid this situation when possible.

DID YOU KNOW?

The biblical titles that are used to address Christ in the O-antiphons are: Wisdom of Our God Most High, Leader of the House of Israel, Root of Jesse's Stem, Key of David, Emmanuel, King and Giver of Law, King of All Nations and Keystone of the Church, Radiant Dawn.

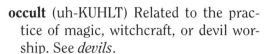

occult (uh-KUHLT) Related to the practice of magic, witchcraft, or devil worship. See *devils*.

octave (OK-tiv) The celebration of a feast on the actual day and for the next seven days. Today only the octaves of Christmas and Easter are observed. *Octave* comes from the Latin word for "eight."

Offertory See *Preparation of Gifts*.

offertory collection (AW-fer-tor-ee kuh-LEK-shuhn) The gathering of donations during the Preparation of the Gifts at Mass for the support of the parish and those in special need.

oils, holy (oils, HOH-lee) Oil that is blessed by the bishop on Holy Thursday and then used in administering several of the  sacraments. The *oil of catechumens* is used in the sacrament of Baptism; *chrism* is used for Baptism, Confirmation, Holy Orders, and the blessing of a church; the *oil of the sick* is used in the Anointing of the Sick. As in ancient times, oil represents healing and special dedication. See *chrism, catechumen*.

Old Testament (TEST-a-ment) (1) The first forty-six books of the Bible that deal with the early history of salvation and come to us from the Jewish people who lived before Christ. The Old Testament begins with a description of creation and then tells of important events in the history of the Jews, the Chosen People, during their long wait for the Messiah. Catholics and Orthodox churches accept more books as divinely inspired than do Jews and Protestants. (2) The sacred covenant (agreement) between God and the Israelites on Mount Sinai. *See p. 87 for a list of Old Testament books.*

omnipotent (om-NIP-uh-tuhnt) All-powerful. God is omnipotent, which means that there is nothing that God can't do.

omnipresent (om-nuh-PREZ-unt) Always present. God is omnipresent in the universe.

omniscient (om-NISH-uhnt) All-knowing. God is omniscient, which means that there is nothing that God doesn't know.

one A mark of the Church that means complete and undivided. The Holy Spirit and the Eucharist make us one. Unity is very important in the Church. Many people, from different backgrounds and parts of the earth, make up the Church. But we are one in charity, in professing the faith taught by the Apostles, in celebrating Mass and the sacraments, and in being governed by the pope and bishops. Our unity reflects the unity of the Trinity: three divine Persons, but one God.

Orders, Holy See *Holy Orders*.

Ordinary Time (OR-dun-er-ee) The liturgical season that spans thirty-four weeks of the Church year. The first part of this season follows the Christmas season and ends with Ash Wednesday. The second part follows the Easter season and ends with the start of Advent.

ordination (or-dn-AY-shuhn) The act of conferring the sacrament of Holy Orders. In this case, one would say that a priest has been "ordained."

original holiness (uh-RIJ-uh-nuhl HOH-lee-nis) Also called original justice. Our first parents' sharing in divine life; harmony within them, between them, and between them and all creation.

original sin See *sin, original*.

Orthodox (OR-thuh-doks) (1) Refers to correct doctrine and worship. (2) Refers to the Eastern Churches that separated from the Western Church in 1054. These Churches can trace their bishops back to the apostles, but they do not recognize the pope as their chief spiritual leader.

Our Father See *Lord's Prayer*.

Our Lady A title given to Mary, the Mother of Jesus, our Lord. In French, it is *Notre Dame*.

pall (pawl) (1) A square of cardboard covered with linen that is placed over the chalice to prevent anything from falling into it. (2) The cloth that is laid over a coffin during a funeral Mass.

papacy (PAY-puh-see) (1) The position or office of the pope. Besides being head of the Church, the pope is also the ruler of Vatican City. (2) The period of time a pope spends in office.

papal bull (PAY-puhl bull) A solemn letter from the pope. The bull got its name from the leaden seal (*bulla* in Latin) that is affixed to the document.

papal definition (def-uh-NISH-uhn) A solemn statement by the pope or an ecumenical council guided by the Holy Spirit that states the meaning of a teaching. Papal definitions are infallible (guaranteed true), and Catholics around the world are required to believe them. See *ecumenical council*.

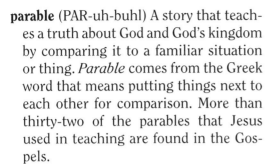

parable (PAR-uh-buhl) A story that teaches a truth about God and God's kingdom by comparing it to a familiar situation or thing. *Parable* comes from the Greek word that means putting things next to each other for comparison. More than thirty-two of the parables that Jesus used in teaching are found in the Gospels.

Paraclete (PAR-uh-kleet) The Holy Spirit, who assists us as our advocate and our counselor. This term is based on a Greek word that describes someone who stands by a person's side to help him or her.

paradise (PAR-uh-dys) (1) The Garden of Eden, where Adam and Eve enjoyed natural happiness until they sinned. (2) Another word for heaven, where we will find complete, supernatural happiness.

parish (PAIR-ish) A community of believers led by a pastor appointed by the bishop and which is part of a diocese. See *diocese*.

parish council (KOUN-suhl) Parishioners elected to assist the pastor in planning and overseeing the activities of the parish.

parishioner (puh-RISH-uh-ner) A person who is a member of a parish.

parousia See *Second Coming*.

particular judgment See *judgment, particular*.

paschal (Easter) **candle** (PAS-kuhl CAN-dul) A large, carved candle symbolizing

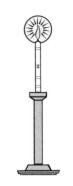

Christ, which is decorated at the Easter Vigil and then lit from the new fire. During the Easter season, the paschal candle is placed near the altar and lit for Mass. After Pentecost, the paschal candle is put near the baptismal font, where the candles of those to be baptized are lit from it. It is also placed near the head of the coffin during a funeral Mass. The candle's light reminds us that the light of Jesus is always stronger than the darkness of sin and death.

paschal mystery (MIS-tuh-ree) The suffering, death, resurrection, and ascension of Jesus. We celebrate this mystery of our salvation at Easter and during the sacraments, in particular during every Mass.

paschal precept (PREE-sept) The rule of the Church that Catholics are to receive Holy Communion at least once a year, usually during the Easter season (in the United States between the first Sunday of Lent and Trinity Sunday). Formerly, when receiving Communion wasn't as common, the Church required everyone to go to confession and receive Communion at least once a year during the Easter season. This was called the "Easter duty."

Passion (PASH-uhn) The sacred and painful events that our Savior went through right before his death.

Passion Sunday The first day of Holy Week, formerly called Palm Sunday, when we commemorate Jesus' entrance into Jerusalem on a donkey. On that day crowds waved palms and shouted, "Hosanna." On Passion Sunday we receive blessed palms to display in our homes.

Passover (PAS-oh-ver) (1) Before the Exodus from Egypt, passover meant that death passed over the Jewish houses marked by the blood of the Lamb. (2) The Jewish feast that celebrates God's saving the Hebrews from death and bringing them to new life in Israel. (3) Jesus' passing over from death to new life, which is celebrated at each Eucharist. See *Exodus*.

pastor (PAS-ter) The priest who is appointed by the bishop to be the one chiefly responsible for the care of the people in a particular parish. The word *pastor* comes from a Latin word that means "shepherd."

paten (PAT-n) A dish, usually of silver or gold, that is used to hold the Host during Mass.

patron saint (PAY-truhn saynt) A special saint who protects and prays for a particular person, parish, diocese, country, or even the whole Church. A person's patron saint is usually the saint he or she has been named after.

penance (PEN-uhns) (1) The virtue that helps a person be sorry for sins, try to avoid sinning again, make up for sin, and return to God, who is eager to forgive. (2) The prayer or good deeds that the priest assigns in the sacrament of Reconciliation to be performed as reparation for sin and a sign of our intention to do better.

Penance, sacrament of (SAK-ruh-muhnt) See *Reconciliation, sacrament of*.

penitent (PEN-i-tuhnt) A person who repents and seeks forgiveness in the sacrament of Reconciliation.

Pentateuch (PEN-tuh-took) The first five books of the Old Testament: Genesis, Exodus, Leviticus, Numbers, and Deuteronomy. The Pentateuch, the collection of the Law, is also called the "Torah."

Pentecost (PEN-ti-kost) (1) The coming of the Holy Spirit to the Church, commonly called the birthday of the Church because it's the day on which the apostles first publicly preached the Good News. The Spirit came with signs of wind and flames on Mary and the apostles while they were praying in Jerusalem. During the Last Supper, Jesus had told his apostles: "The Holy Spirit, whom the Father

will send in my name, will teach you everything, and remind you of all that I have said to you" (John 14:26). The Spirit of Jesus made the apostles brave so that they had the courage to preach fearlessly. (2) The feast fifty days after Easter that celebrates the Holy Spirit's descent upon the Church.

People of God The Church. Christ is the Head of the People of God and the Holy Spirit unites the members. Vatican Council II emphasized this name in its document on the Church, *Dogmatic Constitution on the Church*.

perjury (PUR-juh-ree) The grave sin of lying while under oath. Someone who commits perjury is asking God to witness to a lie.

permanent deacon See *deacon*.

perseverance, final (pur-suh-VEER-uhns) Being in the state of grace at death.

Peter's pence (PEE-terz pents) A special collection taken up each year by the worldwide Church for the purpose of supporting the pope and his projects.

petition (puh-TISH-uhn) A type of prayer in which a person asks for God's blessings.

Pharisees (FAR-uh-seez) An influential group of Jewish laymen, some of whom Jesus scolded for their hypocrisy and pride. The Pharisees were staunch defenders of Jewish law and, unlike the Sadducees, believed in angels and the resurrection of the dead. After the destruction of Jerusalem in A.D. 70, the Pharisees were the ones who preserved Judaism.

piety The gift of the Holy Spirit that helps us love and worship God. It leads to prayer and to a deep respect for God and all God's creation, including other people. See *gifts of the Holy Spirit*.

pilgrimage (PIL-gruh-mij) A journey to a holy place to venerate a saint or to obtain some spiritual favor. A person making a pilgrimage is called a pilgrim.

Pontiff (PON-tif) The Holy Father. *Pontiff* comes from the Latin for "bridge." The pope is a bridge between God and people on earth.

poor souls See *holy souls*.

Pope The visible head of the Church throughout the world, the Vicar of Christ, and the bishop of Rome. The Holy Father is the successor of Saint Peter, who founded the see of Rome.

prayer (prair) Lifting our minds and hearts to God, speaking with God. Prayer can be mental or vocal, done with others or alone. The basic forms of prayer are blessing, petition, intercession, thanksgiving, and praise.

Prayer of the Faithful (FAYTH-fuhl) Petitions offered during Mass for God's blessings on the Church and the world. The Prayer of the Faithful begins and ends with a prayer by the celebrant. It is also called the "general intercessions."

precepts of the Church (PRE-septz) Rules or commandments of the Church that spell out the duties of Catholics. These precepts are considered the bare minimum that Catholics should do if they intend to follow Christ. *See p. 83 for a list of the precepts.*

Preparation of Gifts (prep-uh-RAY-shuhn) The part of the Eucharistic Celebration when bread and wine, which will become Christ's Body and Blood, are brought up  to the altar. The priest prays that God may accept the offerings.

presbyter (prez-bi-ter) See *priest.*

pride The first of the seven capital sins that leads to too much self-esteem and a strong desire to be noticed and honored. People with this kind of pride believe they can rely only on themselves and neglect to give credit to the power and help of God. See *sins, capital.*

priest A baptized man ordained by a bishop with the sacrament of Holy Orders in order to serve the Church as Christ's representative. A priest is given the power to preside at the Eucharist and to absolve sinners. He also baptizes, preaches the Gospel, witnesses mar-

riages, and anoints those who are ill. Priests of the Latin Rite do not marry and usually minister in a parish. (The Eastern Rites, following their ancient tradition, do allow a married man to become a priest, but do not allow a priest to marry *after* being ordained.) There are diocesan priests who are bound to a particular diocese and priests who belong to a religious order or congregation. See *Holy Orders, ordination.*

profanity (pro-FAN-i-tee) The irreverent use of the name of God or one of the saints.

Profession of Faith (proh-FESH-uhn) 1) The public act of declaring faith. 2) The title given to the Creed we pray at Mass.

prophet (PROF-it) One who speaks for God, usually to call people to repentance. The writings and actions of the Old Testament prophets are recorded in the books that bear their names in the Bible. Many prophets were killed for their courage. Jesus is the greatest prophet.

DID YOU KNOW?

The prophets who have books in the Bible named after them are: Isaiah, Jeremiah, Baruch, Ezekiel, Daniel, Hosea, Joel, Amos, Obadiah, Jonah, Micah, Nahum, Habakkuk, Zephaniah, Haggai, Zechariah, and Malachi.

prostration (prah-STRAY-shuhn) A prayer posture in which a person lies on the ground face down in adoration and submission. Priests prostrate during their ordination and in the Good Friday services.

providence See *divine providence*.

prudence (PROOD-ns) The cardinal moral virtue that guides us in making right choices by considering the common good.

Psalms (sahmz) The Old Testament book composed of 150 prayer songs, which tradition says King David wrote. These hymns of praise, which express various feelings, are prayed in the Mass and in the Liturgy of the Hours.

pulpit See *ambo*.

purgatory (PUR-guh-tor-ee) The state of suffering and purification that follows the death of someone who has to make up for sins before entering heaven. If a person dies in the state of grace but still has to atone for sin, he or she goes to purgatory. It's important to pray for the dead so that they can be released from the pain of purgatory sooner, and then go to heaven.

purificator (PYOOR-uh-fi-kay-ter) A small, white linen towel used to wipe the chalice and other sacred vessels after Holy Communion. Usually there is a cross in the center of the purificator.

pyx (piks) The small container used by the priest or Eucharistic minister to bring Holy Communion to the sick.

Queen of Heaven (HEV-uhn) A title given to Mary because she is the Mother of Jesus, who is King of the Universe.

rabbi (RAB-eye) (1) Jewish religious teacher. *Rabbi* comes from the Aramaic word meaning "my master." (2) "Rabbi" was a title of respect used by students addressing their teacher. At times, Jesus was called Rabbi by his followers, although he wasn't officially recognized as one.

Real Presence (REE-uhl PREZ-uhns) The Church teaching that when bread and wine are consecrated by a priest or bishop during the Eucharistic Prayer they become the Body and Blood of Jesus Christ through the power of the Holy Spirit.

Reconciliation, sacrament of (rek-uhn-sil-ee-AY-shuhn) One of the sacraments of healing through which Jesus forgives sins committed after Baptism and reconciles sinners to God and the Church. In this sacrament, we tell our sins to a priest and express our sorrow and our determination to avoid sinning again. The priest assigns a penance (usually a prayer or good deed to perform) and then gives absolution. This sacrament is also referred to as the sacrament of Penance or simply "confession." See *absolution*.

Reconciliation room A room for celebrating the sacrament of Reconciliation. It usually allows for the option of confessing face-to-face or behind a screen.

rectory (REK-tuh-ree) The parish house where the pastor and other priests live.

Redeemer (ri-DEE-mer) Another word for "savior." It refers to Jesus, who ransomed, or bought back, the world from the slavery of sin by his life, death, and resurrection.

redemption (ri-DEMP-shuhn) The deliverance of all of us by Jesus, who became man, suffered, died, and rose to free us from all sin and bring us grace and eternal life.

Regina Caeli (ri-JEE-nuh CHAY-lee) A prayer to Mary used during Eastertime in place of the Angelus. Its title comes from the Latin for the first words of the prayer, "Queen of Heaven." See *Angelus*.

reincarnation (ree-in-kahr-NAY-shuhn) The wrong belief that a dead person's spirit enters another body and lives again. The Church teaches that every person has only one body and soul.

relic (REL-ikz) A saint's body (or part of it), something closely connected to the saint, or something that touched the body of the saint. The Church honors relics. They are placed in shrines and in containers called reliquaries.

A reliquary used to hold a relic.

religion (ri-LIJ-uhn) (1) Belief in God. (2) The virtue by which a person gives God worship and service and fulfills promises made to him.

religious life (ri-LIJ-uhs) Also called consecrated life, a state of life in which men and women are consecrated to God and try to follow Jesus, who was poor, chaste (pure), and obedient. Religious brothers, sisters, and priests usually make vows of poverty, chastity, and obedience. They live together and follow a rule in the spirit of their congregation's founder.

reparation (rep-uh-RAY-shuhn) The act of making up for sin.

repentance (ri-PEN-tuhns) Sorrow for sin and the determination to avoid it in the future.

responsorial psalm (re-sponz-OR-ee-uhl sahm) The psalm prayer, often sung, during the Liturgy of the Word at Mass. A refrain is repeated after sections of the psalm are said or sung.

restitution (res-ti-TOO-shuhn) The act of repairing harm done to another person. To be forgiven for stealing and for hurting a person's reputation, a penitent must make restitution. For example, if someone has stolen something, he or she has to return it, or, if that isn't possible, give something equivalent to charity.

resurrection of Christ (rez-uh-REK-shuhn) Jesus' rising from the dead to new life through his own power on the third day after his death. This is a central belief of our faith.

An artist's conception of the Resurrection.

resurrection of the body The raising of all the dead at the end of the world when the bodies and souls of people will be reunited. Those who are saved will have completely restored, glorious bodies like the risen Jesus has and will be welcomed into heaven.

retreat (ree-TREET) Days of silence and withdrawal from daily activities in order to pray and reflect, usually under the guidance of a director.

revelation (rev-uh-LAY-shuhn) The truths God made known to us about himself and his plans for us through the Bible and Sacred Tradition. God's fullest revelation was his own Son, Jesus Christ. Public revelation ended with the death of the last apostle, Saint John. We are not obliged to believe private revelation, which may be given to individuals through apparitions and other ways. See *Tradition, Sacred; apparition*.

Revelation, Book of The New Testament's final book. It is also called Apocalypse, which is its Greek name. The Book of Revelation was written at a time when Christians were suffering a great deal. These writings were meant to encourage them. Among other things, the author describes various visions. Through figurative language, Revelation tells about the end of the world. The message is clear: despite much suffering, the Church must remain faithful to Jesus, who will come again and who will conquer all enemies.

reverence (REV-er-uhns) See *piety*.

rite (ryt) The words and actions of a liturgical ceremony.

Rite of Christian Initiation of Adults (RCIA) The process through which candidates preparing for full communion with the Catholic Church are instructed in the faith and provided spiritual formation in preparation for the reception of the sacraments of Baptism, Eucharist, and Confirmation.

Roman Catholic (RO-mahn KATH-uh-lik) A member of the Church founded by Jesus Christ and led by the pope, the bishop of Rome and successor of Saint Peter.

Roman Curia (KYOOR-ee-uh) The Church's administrative agencies at the Vatican. They consist of the secretary of state and nine congregations, each dealing with a different aspect of the Church's life.

Rosary (ROH-zuh-ree) (1) A prayer honoring Mary, during which we think about events in the lives of Jesus and Mary while we pray Hail Marys. These events are divided into the Joyful, Sorrowful, Luminous, and Glorious mysteries. A decade of the Rosary is prayed for  each mystery. A decade is made up of an Our Father, ten Hail Marys, and the Glory Be to the Father. (2) The blessed circle of beads on which the prayers of the Rosary are prayed. *See p. 85 for the mysteries.*

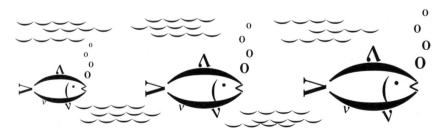

Sabbath (SAB-uhth) The seventh day of the week, Saturday, when Jews rested as God did after creating the universe in six days. Christians celebrate the first day of the week as the Lord's day because it was on a Sunday that Jesus rose from the dead and that the Holy Spirit came on Pentecost. We make Sundays special by participating in the Eucharistic Celebration, praying extra, performing acts of charity, spending time with our families, and doing something other than normal work.

sacramental (sak-ruh-MEN-tl) A holy action or object approved by the Church and used in asking for God's blessings. Sacramentals are similar to sacraments in that they are sacred signs that bring about good through the prayers of the Church.

sacramental character (KAR-ik-ter) The permanent, spiritual quality a person receives at the reception of the sacraments of Baptism, Confirmation, and Holy Orders. These sacraments cannot be repeated.

Sacramentary (sak-ruh-MEN-tah-ree) The official book that contains the prayers used at Mass.

sacraments (SAK-ruh-muhntz) The seven main means that Jesus instituted and entrusted to the Church to give us grace and make us holy. The sacraments are visible signs of what takes place spiritually. Each one gives a special sacramental grace. The sacraments are categorized into three groups: sacraments of initiation or beginning (Baptism, Confirmation, and Holy Eucharist),

Did You Know?

Some of the most common sacramentals are: holy water, ashes, priest's blessing, rosary beads, statues, medals, scapulars, candles, holy pictures, crosses, crucifixes, making the sign of the cross, chrism, and other holy oils.

sacraments of healing (Reconciliation and the Anointing of the Sick), and sacraments at the service of communion (Holy Orders and Matrimony).

Sacred Heart of Jesus (SAY-krid) A symbol of Christ's love for humanity. This divine love is what moved Jesus to freely give his life so that we could be saved. In art, the Sacred Heart is pictured with thorns wrapped around it and flames coming from it. These images remind us that Jesus suffered a great deal during his passion and death. It takes a heart on fire with love to make such a sacrifice. See *First Fridays*.

A statue portraying the Sacred Heart of Jesus

Sacred Scripture See *Bible*.

Sacred Tradition See *Tradition, Sacred*.

sacred writers The human writers who composed the books of the Bible under the inspiration of the Holy Spirit.

sacrifice (SAK-ruh-fys) (1) An offering made to God by a priest out of adoration, thanksgiving, supplication, or penance. (2) An act of self-denial done out of love for God, for example, giving up candy or, instead of watching TV, helping with dishes.

sacrilege (SAK-ruh-lij) The sin of disrespectfully treating a sacred person, place, or thing that is related to God.

For example, it is a sacrilege to receive Holy Communion while not in the state of grace.

sacristy (SAK-ri-stee) A room near the sanctuary of a church used for storing the sacred vessels, vestments, and supplies needed for the celebration of the liturgy. Priests and deacons put on and take off their vestments in the sacristy.

Sadducees (SADJ-yoo-seez) Wealthy, educated Jewish leaders, perhaps priests and their supporters, at the time of Jesus. The Sadducees rejected the idea of life after death and did not believe in angels. They considered only the Torah and not the writings of the prophets to be Sacred Scripture. See *Torah, Pentateuch*.

saints (1) People whom the Church has canonized, thereby telling us that they lived holy lives and are worthy of public veneration and imitation. (2) All those who served God on earth and are now enjoying their reward in heaven. They pray for us. (3) According to Saint Paul, *all those*—even the living—who follow Christ and live in his grace. See *canonization*.

salvation (sal-VAY-shuhn) Deliverance from the bonds of sin that lead to eternal punishment. Through his passion, death, and resurrection, Jesus saved us from sin so we could go to heaven.

Salve Regina (SAHL-vay ri-JEE-nuh) A prayer that honors Mary as our Queen. The prayer's name comes from its first

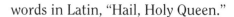

words in Latin, "Hail, Holy Queen."

sanctifying grace See *grace, sanctifying*.

sanctity (SANK-ti-tee) Holiness, sharing in God's life. Sanctity is present in a person who possesses grace.

sanctuary (SANK-choo-er-ee) The most sacred part of the church where the altar and probably the tabernacle are located and the Eucharist is celebrated. The sanctuary is usually higher than the rest of the church and specially decorated.

sanctuary lamp A lamp in the sanctuary that reminds believers of the Real Presence of Jesus in the Holy Eucharist. The lamp is lit whenever the Blessed Sacrament is present.

Sanhedrin (san-HED-rin) The most powerful court and governing body in the ancient Jewish nation. The Sanhedrin had twenty-one members and was led by the high priest.

Satan See *devils*.

Savior (SAYV-yer) The Redeemer, Jesus Christ, who freed people from bondage to sin.

scandal (SKAN-dl) An evil action or omission that directly or indirectly leads another to sin.

scapular (SKAP-yuh-ler) (1) Two strips of cloth joined across the shoulders and covering front and back that form part

of the habit of some religious orders. (2) Two small pieces of cloth connected by strings that are worn around the neck in front and in back in imitation of a scapular of a religious habit. They are a sign of association with the spirituality of a particular religious order. Scapulars are sacramentals that have indulgences connected with them.

scapular medal (MED-uhl) A medal with the Sacred Heart on one side and the Blessed Virgin on the other that may be worn as a substitute for a scapular after a person has been invested in the cloth one.

schism (SKIZ-uhm) The sin of deliberately breaking away from the Church. This term comes from the Greek word meaning "split."

scribes Jewish scholars and government officials who studied the Law of Moses, explained it to the people, and enforced its observance. Most of the scribes were Pharisees.

Scripture, Sacred See *Bible*.

scruple (SKROO-puhl) A needless fear that something is sinful when it is not, often accompanied by feelings of guilt and anxiety.

seal of confession (kuhn-FESH-uhn) The serious obligation a priest has to never repeat anything he learns while hearing a confession.

Second Coming (SEK-uhnd KUHM-ing) The appearance of Christ in majesty at the end of the world when he will come to judge it.

Second Vatican Council An ecumenical council that met at the Vatican from 1962–1965. It brought about major changes in the liturgy and in other areas of Catholic life. See *ecumenical council*.

seminary (SEM-uh-ner-ee) The place where men train to become priests.

seraphim (SER-uh-fim) The highest of the nine choirs of angels. The Bible mentions them in the book of Isaiah, chapter 6. They serve and glorify God. See *cherubim, angels*.

sermon (SUR-muhn) A talk given by a member of the clergy to instruct listeners about religion. The sermon given after the Gospel at Mass is called a homily.

Sign of the Cross The prayer through which we express our belief in the Trinity and in the redemption from sin that Jesus won for us. While praying the words, "In the name of the Father, and of the Son, and of the Holy Spirit," we trace on ourselves a cross by touching our forehead, chest, and each shoulder. We begin and end prayers with the Sign of the Cross and blessings are given with it.

sin, actual (AK-choo-uhl) A free act in which a person chooses to do what God has forbidden. Actual sin can be venial or mortal.

sin, mortal (MOR-tl) A serious offense against God's law that destroys the life of grace in the soul and deprives a person of the right to eternal happiness in heaven. To commit a mortal sin, three things are necessary: the matter of the sin has to be serious, the person must clearly know that the act is evil, and the person must give free and full consent to the evil being done. To be forgiven, the person must repent and receive the sacrament of Reconciliation.

sin, original (uh-RIJ-uh-nl) (1) The offense committed by our first parents, Adam and Eve, in the garden of Eden; the first sin. (2) The state of being born without sanctifying grace and with a tendency to sin that we experience as a result of our first parents' sin.

sin, venial (VEE-nee-uhl) Disobedience to God either in a lesser matter or in a serious matter but without full knowledge, freedom, or consent. Venial sin does not destroy our friendship with God, but it does weaken that friendship. It also makes it harder for us to become holy and may lead to more serious sin.

sins, capital (KAP-i-tl) The seven sins that are the sources of other sins: pride, avarice, envy, wrath, lust, gluttony, and sloth. These are also called vices and the "deadly sins." They are the opposite of the capital virtues. See *virtues, capital*.

sins, social (SOH-shuhl) Sins that corrupt society and for which all are responsible, such as racism and poverty.

sister, religious A woman consecrated to God by vows, usually the vows of poverty, chastity, and obedience. A sister belongs to a religious order or congregation with a particular mission and ordinarily lives in community.

slander (SLAN-der) The sin of damaging someone's reputation by telling lies, leaving out important facts, or telling something that is true but harmful to a person's reputation.

sloth Laziness that keeps someone from praying, working, or fulfilling some other duty. Sloth is one of the seven capital sins. If sloth prevents a person from fulfilling an important obligation, it can be seriously wrong.

social justice (SOH-shuhl JUHS-tis) The responsibility of all Catholics to fight against social sin by working to see that all people are treated with dignity, have their rights protected and their basic needs met. For example, all people should have food, good water, clothing, shelter, and enough money to live on.

solemnity (suh-LEM-ni-tee) The highest rank of liturgical celebration. Of less importance is a feast and of least importance is an optional memorial.

Son of God This title is used to describe the divine sonship of Jesus, who is the Son of the Father. The title declares the fact that Jesus Christ is truly both God and man.

Son of Man Jesus used this title to describe himself; it indicates his divine authority and his unique mission.

soul, human (sohl, HYOO-muhn) The spiritual, immortal part of a human being that gives life to the body. Together, soul and body make up the person. God creates each soul and infuses it into the body. When the body dies, the soul still lives. It will be reunited with the body on the last day.

spirit (SPIR-it) (1) A living, nonmaterial being. (2) The soul, life force, supernatural life.

spiritual works of mercy Acts of charity that are performed for those who have a spiritual need. *See p. 84 for a list of the spiritual works of mercy.*

sponsor (SPON-ser) A person who at someone's Baptism or Confirmation agrees to assist that person in living out the Catholic faith.

Stations of the Cross (STAY-shuhnz) Prayers said while remembering fourteen painful incidents during the passion and death of Jesus. The actual "stations" are small crosses hung on the walls of churches. They are usually accompanied by artwork that corresponds to each event Jesus experienced. (Some churches or shrines also have outdoor Stations of the Cross.) People walk from station to station as they pray. This devotion is also called the Way of the Cross. It originated because not everyone could go to Jerusalem to walk the actual way of the cross that Jesus walked. *See p. 86 for the Stations of the Cross.*

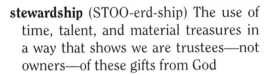

stewardship (STOO-erd-ship) The use of time, talent, and material treasures in a way that shows we are trustees—not owners—of these gifts from God

stigmata (stig-MAH-tuh) Phenomenon in which a person unexplainably bears the wounds of Christ in his or her body. Saint Francis of Assisi and Saint Padre Pio are two well-known stigmatists.

stipend (STY-pend) A donation made to a priest for a special service, such as celebrating a Mass.

stole A long, narrow cloth that bishops and priests wear around their necks and deacons wear over their left shoulders for liturgical celebrations.

suffrages (SUHF-ri-jez) Prayers—including Masses—offered for the dead or for other special intentions.

Sunday obligation (ob-li-GAY-shuhn) The duty that Catholics have to participate at Mass on Sundays and holy days of obligation. They may also fulfill this obligation by participating in Mass on Saturday night.

supernatural (soo-per-NACH-er-uhl) Above and beyond what is natural. Grace, for example, is a supernatural gift of God. We would not naturally possess grace if God did not choose to give it to us.

supernatural adoption See *adoption, supernatural.*

surplice (SUR-plis) A loose white vestment of half length that is worn by clergy and sometimes laity who are serving in a liturgical ceremony.

synod (SIN-uhd) A meeting of bishops from all over the world called by the pope to share information and experiences and discuss concerns on a particular topic. The synod of bishops was instituted in 1965 to keep alive the spirit of the Second Vatican Council.

tabernacle (TAB-er-nak-uhl) A container for the Holy Eu-charist for the purposes of bringing Holy Communion to the sick and for adoration and prayer. The tabernacle is located either in the sanctuary or in a side chapel of the church.

temperance (TEM-per-uhns) A cardinal virtue that gives a person self-control. A person with temperance is able to control the urge for pleasure so that it doesn't get out of hand.

temple (TEM-puhl) (1) A Jewish building dedicated to worship and sacrifice. King Solomon built the first Temple in Jerusalem, and this was rebuilt twice before being completely destroyed by the Romans in A.D. 70. (2) A building where God is present. Members of the Church are also temples of the Holy Spirit, who dwells in them.

temptation (temp-TAY-shuhn) Something that urges us to sin and makes sin seem good. The source may be another person or thing, our own desires, or the devil. Every human being is tempted—even Jesus was. When we conquer temptation, we refuse to disobey God's law. When we give in to temptation, we sin. It's important to pray when we feel tempted to think, say, or do something forbidden by God.

testament (TES-tuh-muhnt) An agreement or covenant.

thanksgiving (thangks-GIV-ing) A type of prayer in which we acknowledge the many gifts God has given us and express gratitude for them.

theological virtues (thee-uh-LOJ-i-kuhl VUR-chooz) Faith, hope, and love. They are called "theological" because they are given to us by God, and they lead us to believe, trust, and love God.

theology (thee-OL-uh-jee) The study of God, revelation, and the way these truths relate to other knowledge. Theology is often described as "faith seeking understanding."

thurible See *censer*.

tithe (tyth) The act of giving to God a part of what one earns. The Old Testament refers to tithing as giving 10 percent to God. It is a precept of the Church that Catholics contribute what they can to support the work of the Church.

Torah See *Pentateuch*.

Tower of Babel See *Babel, Tower of*

Tradition, Sacred (truh-DISH-uhn, SAY-krid) The collection of Jesus' teachings that were not written down right away by the early Christians. Instead, these truths were passed down under the inspiration of the Holy Spirit from the apostles through their successors, the bishops. Later on, tradition was written down, especially in the official teachings of the Church. Catholics consider the Bible and Sacred Tradition to be God's revelation, the Deposit of Faith. See *Deposit of Faith*.

Transfiguration (trans-fig-yuh-RAY-shuhn) The wondrous event of Jesus letting Peter, James, and John witness his divine glory. Moses and Elijah appeared with Jesus and spoke with him of his coming death and resurrection.

transitional deacon See *deacon*.

transubstantiation (tran-suhb-stan-shee-AY-shuhn) The complete, unique change of bread and wine into the Body and Blood of Jesus. Transubstantiation takes place at Mass during the Eucharistic Prayer. Afterwards, the bread and wine look, feel, smell, and taste the same, but they have actually become the Body and Blood of Christ. The substances have changed. This is a mystery of faith.

Trappists (TRAP-istz) Members of the Cistercian Order, who follow a rule established by an abbey in France in 1664. Trappists are known for their silence and life of penance.

triduum (TRID-oo-uhm) (1) A three-day period devoted to prayer and related to some special feast day. (2) In particular, the Easter Triduum, the three days after Lent beginning with the Mass of the Lord's Supper on Holy Thursday and concluding with Evening Prayer on Easter Sunday.

Trinity, Holy (TRIN-i-tee) The one true God, who is three Persons with one nature. We call the three Persons the Father, the Son, and the Holy Spirit. This mystery is central to our Catholic faith.

DID YOU KNOW?

The Holy Trinity has long been depicted in sacred art and teaching through the use of various symbols. In his preaching to the pagan Celts of Ireland in the fifth century, Saint Patrick used the shamrock. He explained the mystery of three Persons in one God by showing them the shamrock plant, which has one leaf with three lobes.

understanding (uhn-der-STAND-ing) The gift of the Holy Spirit that gives insight into the truths of the faith. It enables a person to know the meaning and consequences of what God has revealed.

United States Conference of Catholic Bishops (USCCB) The organization of all the United States bishops working together to carry out activities in the United States. The headquarters of the conference is in Washington, D.C. The bishops produce documents on timely topics and meet twice a year.

unity See *one*.

universal judgment After the final resurrection of all the dead, the entire human race will stand in judgment before Jesus Christ. Each person's deeds will be made known in a way that will show how we have affected the lives of others for good or for evil.

Vatican City (VAT-i-kuhn CIT-ee) The small, independent country with a population of nearly one thousand that is governed by the pope. Even though Vatican City is situated on only about 108 acres of land, it is very important to Catholics and to the world. Here are located the residence of the Holy Father, as well as many Church offices and museums. Saint Peter's Basilica, the sec-

ond largest Christian church in the world, is also located in Vatican City.

Vatican Council II (KOUN-suhl) The ecumenical (worldwide) meeting of bishops held from 1962 to 1965 that Pope John XXIII called to bring the Church into the modern world. About 2,500 bishops took part in this council, which produced sixteen documents.

Venerable (VEN-er-uh-buhl) A Church title given to a deceased person who is being considered for canonization but has not yet been named "Blessed." A person with the title Venerable has lived a life of heroic virtue.

veneration (ven-uh-RAY-shuhn) The honor given to Mary and the saints. This honor does not equal the worship or adoration we give only to God. See *adoration*.

venial sin See *sin, venial*.

vestments (VEST-muhntz) The special clothing worn by clergy during liturgical services.

Viaticum (vy-AT-i-kuhm) The Holy Eucharist received by someone who is dying. This Latin term means "with you on the way." Through Viaticum, a person has Jesus as a companion on the journey from earthly to heavenly life. He or she is also nourished and strengthened for the journey.

Vicar of Christ (VIK-er) The Holy Father or pope, who takes Jesus' place on earth.

vice A practice or habit that leads a person to sin.

vigil (VIJ-uhl) The day or eve before an important feast.

vigil light A candle lit for a special intention or as an act of devotion, usually in a shrine or church and commonly near a sacred image. The flame stands for the prayers  of the person who lit the candle even after that person leaves.

vigil Mass A Eucharistic Celebration on Saturday evening using the readings and prayers for Sunday. This Mass fulfills the Sunday obligation and is based on the Hebrew view that Sabbaths and feast days begin at sundown of the previous day.

virgin birth Through the power of the Holy Spirit, Mary's virginity when she conceived and gave birth to Jesus. The virgin birth teaches us the divinity of Jesus because his only Father is God.

Virgin Mary (VUR-jin) The Mother of God, Mary of Nazareth. Her son Jesus was conceived through the power of the Holy Spirit and had no human father. That Mary remained a virgin before, during, and after the birth of Jesus is a dogma of the Catholic faith.

virtue (VUR-choo) The habit of doing something good and pleasing to God. See *cardinal virtues; theological virtues; virtues, capital*.

virtues, capital (KAP-i-tl) The seven good habits that are contrary to the seven capital sins: humility, generosity, chastity, meekness, temperance, love of others, and diligence.

Visitation of Mary (viz-i-TAY-shuhn) The journey of Mary to help her elderly relative Elizabeth. When the Angel Gabriel appeared to Mary to announce that she had been chosen to be the Mother of Jesus, he also told her that Elizabeth was going  to be a mother soon, too. When Mary arrived, the baby within Elizabeth leaped for joy. This was the first "meeting" between the unborn sons, Jesus and John the Baptist. The Church celebrates the feast of the Visitation on May 31 and also remembers this occasion as the Second Joyful Mystery of the Rosary.

vocation (voh-KAY-shuhn) God's call of a person to a certain way of life. Everyone is called to holiness and achieves it through the particular state of life he or she is called to: marriage, single life, the ordained life of a priest or deacon, or the religious life. A person can also be called to a certain career, ministry, or service.

vow A sacred promise made to God. When someone makes a vow, he or she freely pledges to live a certain way or perform a certain act that is pleasing to God.

Way of the Cross See *Stations of the Cross*.

will of God (1) God's loving plan for our lives. (2) What God asks us to do, for example, to obey the commandments.

wisdom (WIZ-duhm) (1) The gift of the Holy Spirit that is the ability to put God first, to love the things of God, and to see things from God's point of view and therefore to make good judgments. (2) A book of the Old Testament. (3) Another name for Jesus, the Word of God.

wise men See *Magi*.

witness (WIT-nis) Giving testimony to

truths of the faith by one's words and actions. Bearing witness to Christ and his way of life sometimes calls for courage.

Word of God In a general sense, this refers to God's revelation given to the prophets and especially through Jesus, who is called the Word of God. This term can also refer specifically to the Bible.

works of mercy See *corporal works of mercy, spiritual works of mercy*.

worship Adoration, honor, and praise given to God, especially in the Church's liturgy.

Yahweh (YAH-way) The personal name of God in Hebrew. God revealed this sacred name to Moses when he spoke to him from the burning bush. See *Lord*.

Zion (ZY-uhn) A name for Jerusalem.

zucchetto (zoo-KET-oh) The small, round skullcap worn by the pope, cardinals, bishops, and abbots. The color of the zucchetto indicates the rank of the wearer. For example, the pope wears white and the cardinals wear scarlet.

*For Your Information

The 10 Commandments

1. I, the Lord, am your God: you shall not have strange gods before me.

2. You shall not take the name of the Lord your God in vain.

3. Remember to keep holy the Lord's day.

4. Honor your father and your mother.

5. You shall not kill.

6. You shall not commit adultery.

7. You shall not steal.

8. You shall not bear false witness against your neighbor.

9. You shall not covet your neighbor's wife.

10. You shall not covet your neighbor's goods.

The Beatitudes

"Blessed are the poor in spirit, for theirs is the kingdom of heaven.

Blessed are those who mourn, for they will be comforted.

Blessed are the meek, for they will inherit the earth.

Blessed are those who hunger and thirst for righteousness, for they will be filled.

Blessed are the merciful, for they will receive mercy.

Blessed are the pure in heart, for they will see God.

Blessed are the peacemakers, for they will be called children of God.

Blessed are those who are persecuted for righteousness' sake, for theirs is the kingdom of heaven." (Matthew 5:3–10)

The Sacraments

Sacraments of Initiation:
Baptism, Confirmation, Eucharist

Sacraments of Healing:
Penance, Anointing of the Sick

Sacraments at the Service of Communion:
Holy Orders, Matrimony

Holy Days of Obligation

Mary, Mother of God—January 1 (except when it falls on a Saturday or Monday)

Ascension of Our Lord—the Thursday forty days after Easter, or in some dioceses, the Sunday before Pentecost

Assumption of the Blessed Virgin Mary—August 15 (except when it falls on a Saturday or Monday)

All Saints' Day—November 1 (except when it falls on a Saturday or Monday)

Mary's Immaculate Conception—December 8

Christmas—December 25

Unless otherwise designated, the holy days of obligation in Canada are:

Mary, Mother of God—January 1

Christmas—December 25

Precepts of the Church

★ Observe Sundays and holy days of obligation by participating in Mass and avoiding unnecessary work.

★ Lead a sacramental life, at least once a year receiving Communion (preferably during the Easter season) and confessing grave sins.

★ Fast and abstain on the days appointed by the Church.

★ Provide for the material needs of the Church, according to one's ability.

★ Follow the Church's marriage law and teach one's children about the Catholic faith.

★ Throughout life, learn about the Catholic faith, especially when preparing to receive a sacrament.

★ Take part in the missionary work of the Church and pray for those in need throughout the world.

Corporal Works of Mercy

Feed the hungry.
Give drink to the thirsty.
Clothe the naked.
Visit the imprisoned.
Shelter the homeless.
Visit the sick.
Bury the dead.

Spiritual Works of Mercy

Admonish the sinner.
Instruct the ignorant.
Counsel the doubtful.
Comfort the sorrowful.
Bear wrongs patiently.
Forgive all injuries.
Pray for the living and the dead.

The Seven Capital (Deadly) Sins

Pride   Avarice

Envy   Wrath

Lust   Gluttony

Sloth

The Theological Virtues

Faith
Hope
Charity (love)

The Cardinal Virtues

Prudence
Justice
Fortitude
Temperance

The Gifts
of the Holy Spirit

Wisdom
Understanding
Counsel
Fortitude
Knowledge
Piety
Fear of the Lord

The Fruits
of the Holy Spirit

Charity
Peace
Kindness
Generosity
Faithfulness
Self-control

Joy
Patience
Goodness
Gentleness
Modesty
Chastity

Mysteries of the Rosary

The Joyful Mysteries
1. The Annunciation
2. The Visitation
3. The Birth of Jesus
4. The Presentation in the Temple
5. The Finding of the Child Jesus in the Temple

The Luminous Mysteries
1. The Baptism of Jesus at the Jordan
2. The Miracle at Cana
3. The Proclamation of the Kingdom of God and the Call to Conversion
4. The Transfiguration of Jesus
5. The Institution of the Eucharist

The Sorrowful Mysteries
1. The Agony in the Garden
2. The Scourging at the Pillar
3. The Crowning with Thorns
4. The Carrying of the Cross
5. The Crucifixion and Death of Jesus

The Glorious Mysteries
1. The Resurrection
2. The Ascension
3. The Descent of the Holy Spirit at Pentecost
4. The Assumption of Mary
5. The Crowning of the Blessed Virgin as Queen of Heaven and Earth

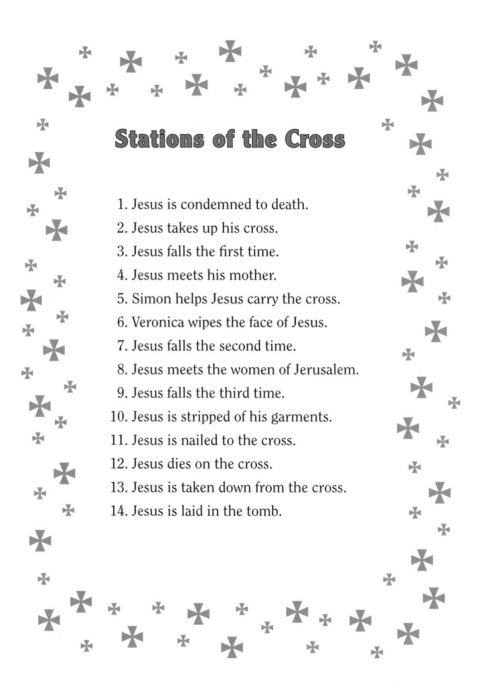

Stations of the Cross

1. Jesus is condemned to death.
2. Jesus takes up his cross.
3. Jesus falls the first time.
4. Jesus meets his mother.
5. Simon helps Jesus carry the cross.
6. Veronica wipes the face of Jesus.
7. Jesus falls the second time.
8. Jesus meets the women of Jerusalem.
9. Jesus falls the third time.
10. Jesus is stripped of his garments.
11. Jesus is nailed to the cross.
12. Jesus dies on the cross.
13. Jesus is taken down from the cross.
14. Jesus is laid in the tomb.

Books of the Bible

The Old Testament

The Pentateuch

Genesis, Exodus, Leviticus, Numbers, Deuteronomy

The Historical Books

Joshua, Judges, Ruth, 1 Samuel, 2 Samuel, 1 Kings, 2 Kings, 1 Chronicles, 2 Chronicles, Ezra, Nehemiah, Tobit, Judith, Esther, 1 Maccabees, 2 Maccabees

The Wisdom Books

Job, Psalms, Proverbs, Ecclesiastes, Song of Songs, Wisdom, Sirach

The Prophetic Books

Isaiah, Jeremiah, Lamentations, Baruch, Ezekiel, Daniel, Hosea, Joel, Amos, Obadiah, Jonah, Micah, Nahum, Habakkuk, Zephaniah, Haggai, Zechariah, Malachi

The New Testament

The Gospels and Acts

Matthew, Mark, Luke, John, Acts of the Apostles

The Epistles

Romans, 1 Corinthians, 2 Corinthians, Galatians, Ephesians, Philippians, Colossians, 1 Thessalonians, 2 Thessalonians, 1 Timothy, 2 Timothy, Titus, Philemon, Hebrews, James, 1 Peter, 2 Peter, 1 John, 2 John, 3 John, Jude

The Book of Revelation

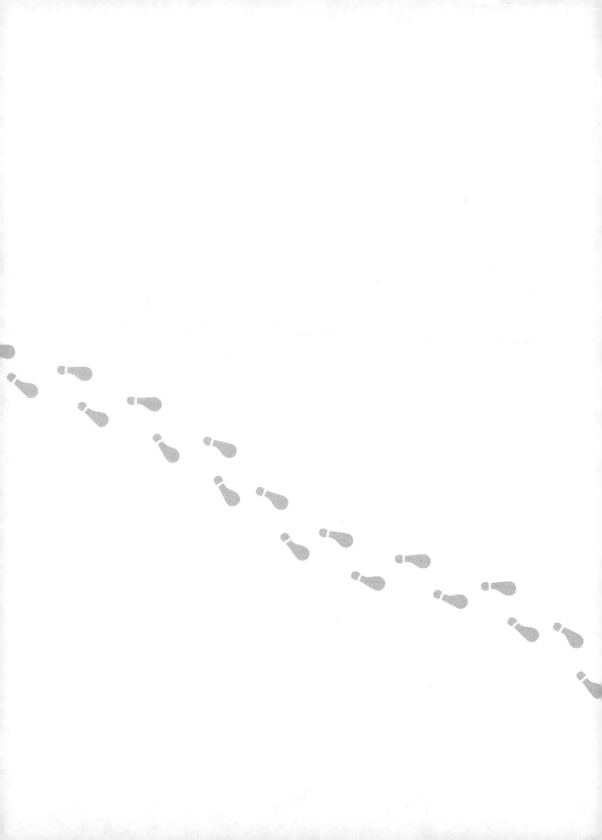

Experience the adventures and challenges,

heroism and holiness of some of the greatest friends of God!

The saints live and breathe again in these stories you won't want to put down. Each book in this ongoing series also features a special prayer and a glossary of terms. Collect them all, and meet the saints!

**Price: $7.95
($9.95 Canadian)
1-800-876-4463
www.pauline.org**

Encounter the Saints Series

Blesseds Jacinta and Francisco Marto
Shepherds of Fatima

Blessed Pier Giorgio Frassati
Journey to the Summit

Blessed Teresa of Calcutta
Missionary of Charity

Journeys with Mary
Apparitions of Our Lady

Saint Anthony of Padua
Fire and Light

Saint Bakhita of Sudan
Forever Free

Saint Bernadette Soubirous
Light in the Grotto

Saint Edith Stein
Blessed by the Cross

Saint Elizabeth Ann Seton
Daughter of America

Saint Faustina Kowalska
Messenger of Mercy

Saint Frances Xavier Cabrini
Cecchina's Dream

Saint Francis of Assisi
Gentle Revolutionary

Saint Ignatius of Loyola
For the Greater Glory of God

Saint Isaac Jogues
With Burning Heart

Saint Joan of Arc
God's Soldier

Saint Juan Diego
And Our Lady of Guadalupe

Saint Katharine Drexel
The Total Gift

Saint Martin de Porres
Humble Healer

Saint Maximilian Kolbe
Mary's Knight

Saint Paul
The Thirteenth Apostle

Saint Pio of Pietrelcina
Rich in Love

Saint Thérèse of Lisieux
The Way of Love

Pauline
BOOKS & MEDIA

BOOKS & MEDIA

The Daughters of St. Paul operate book and media centers at the following addresses.
Visit, call or write the one nearest you today,
or find us on the World Wide Web, www.pauline.org

CALIFORNIA
3908 Sepulveda Blvd, Culver City, CA 90230   310-397-8676
2640 Broadway Street, Redwood City, CA 94063   650-369-4230
5945 Balboa Avenue, San Diego, CA 92111   858-565-9181

FLORIDA
145 S.W. 107th Avenue, Miami, FL 33174   305-559-6715

HAWAII
1143 Bishop Street, Honolulu, HI 96813   808-521-2731
Neighbor Islands call: 866-521-2731

ILLINOIS
172 North Michigan Avenue, Chicago, IL 60601   312-346-4228

LOUISIANA
4403 Veterans Memorial Blvd, Metairie, LA 70006   504-887-7631

MASSACHUSETTS
885 Providence Hwy, Dedham, MA 02026   781-326-5385

MISSOURI
9804 Watson Road, St. Louis, MO 63126   314-965-3512

NEW JERSEY
561 U.S. Route 1, Wick Plaza, Edison, NJ 08817   732-572-1200

NEW YORK
Relocating. Please call: 212-754-1110

PENNSYLVANIA
9171-A Roosevelt Blvd, Philadelphia, PA 19114   215-676-9494

SOUTH CAROLINA
243 King Street, Charleston, SC 29401   843-577-0175

VIRGINIA
1025 King Street, Alexandria, VA 22314   703-549-3806

CANADA
3022 Dufferin Street, Toronto, ON M6B 3T5   416-781-9131